Y0-CAR-262

Mt. McKinley Mutual Savings Bank

is proud to make possible the limited edition of this book entitled, *FAIRBANKS: A PICTORIAL HISTORY*. This beautiful illustrated and carefully documented volume will prove a valuable addition to your family library and a collector's item for years to come.

On behalf of the trustees, officers and employees of Mt. McKinley Mutual Savings Bank, I am pleased to dedicate this book to the thousands of families and individuals and their descendants who have made this history.

K.G. Thompson

K.G. Thompson, President
& Chief Executive Officer

Fairbanks
A PICTORIAL HISTORY
CLAUS-M. NASKE and L. J. ROWINSKI

design by Jamie Backus Raynor

The Donning Company/Publishers
Norfolk / Virginia Beach

Copyright © 1981 by Claus-M. Naske and L. J. Rowinski

All rights reserved, including the right to
reproduce this book in any form whatsoever
without permission in writing from the
publisher, except for brief passages in
connection with a review. For information,
write: The Donning Company/Publishers,
5659 Virginia Beach Boulevard, Norfolk,
Virginia 23502

**Library of Congress Cataloging in
Publication Data**
Naske, Claus-M.
Fairbanks, a pictorial history.
Bibliography: p.
Includes index.
1. Fairbanks, Alaska—Decription—Views.
2. Fairbanks, Alaska—History—Pictorial
works.
I. Rowinski, Ludwig J., 1929- joint author. II.
Title.
F914.F16N37   979.8'6   80-27429
ISBN 0-89865-108-5 (pbk.)   AACR1

Printed in the United States of America

Contents

Foreword

The founding of Fairbanks was an accident, involving a river too shallow and a chance meeting between trader E. T. Barnette and prospector Felix Pedro. Fairbanks, from the beginning, was not a gold mining camp, but rather a trading post providing supplies to prospectors and miners in the Tanana Valley.

Most of the gold camps that sprang up in the valley are now gone, but Fairbanks, still a vital supply center, persists and today is a modern community, the second largest in the State, with amenities appropriate to a town three or four times its population of thirty thousand.

The story of how a tiny trading post evolved into a university city of science, scholarship, and culture is told beautifully in *Fairbanks: A Pictorial History.* It is the story of people, some who came for gold, and others who came to provide supplies and services for those who were working the creeks.

Ingenious, adaptable, independent, self-reliant, they found ways to cope with isolation, with extremes of environment, with natural disasters, with frustrations, and endless physical hardships.

Lured by the richness of the resources at hand, they fell in love with the natural beauty, the vastness and grandeur of the land, perhaps its very loneliness, and they stayed. The found strength in one another and became a close-knit, self-contained community while stressing individuality, a splendid example of unity amid diversity. And they lived with gusto!

Historian Claus M. Naske and museum administrator Ludwig J. Rowinski have combined their talents and enthusiasm to present the story of Fairbanks with rare insight into the lives of the people who founded and built the community. Their day-to-day activities and interests, their aspirations and accomplishments are recorded with understanding and compassion. We see the people at work for themselves, their families, their town and country, involved in school, in church, in cultural activities, in sports, and in civic gatherings. Commonplace, ordinary people? Perhaps, but performing extraordinarily under adversity and responding positively to opportunity. Such is the essence historically of greatness, which they did not seek but lived.

All this and much more has been captured by the

authors who themselves have been active participants in the growth and development of Fairbanks. The account of the people and their community is not a typical pictorial history with a few captions and a bit of text surrounding pictures. It is an excellent interpretative historical overview lavishly illustrated. It is a sourcebook of fascinating information. Even the trivia illustrates the past. Theirs is a comprehensive and detailed presentation of the way Fairbanks developed into the town it is today.

In few other pioneer settlements were there three daily newspapers, two breweries, two hospitals, a foundry, a river-boat shipyard, a public elementary and secondary school, a library, numerous greenhouses, an outdoor swimming pool enjoyed by all though privately owned, and a woman attorney, the wife of a local dentist. And this in 1908 or thereabouts at nearly sixty-five degrees North!

From dog-sled mail routes to the first bush pilot airmail route to polar exploration, from fires and floods to military construction to oil exploration and the good and bad aspects of the impact of building an eight hundred mile pipeline that skirts the city's boundaries—it is all here to enjoy, to stir nostalgic memories, and perhaps to serve as inspiration.

Apparently many residents of Fairbanks had cameras and used them from the earliest days. The wealth of material available in the archives of the University of Alaska and in private collections extant must have challenged the authors and made their task of selection a difficult one. Both the quality of the photographs and their social and historical significance are exceptional.

The wealth of material available would provide for a number of books, but congratulations clearly are in order for the authors and all who participated in bringing to the public a delightful and significant account of the past in *Fairbanks: A Pictorial History.*

William Ransom Wood
Fairbanks Mayor 1978-80
President, Fairbanks
Industrial Development
Corporation, 1973 to 1980
President, University of
Alaska, 1960-1973.

Acknowledgments

In eighty years, Fairbanks has grown from a reluctant stop on a river bank to a thriving modern community. Photography had come of age by the turn of the century and everything was worth recording on film. The earliest photos of primitive cabins in the wilderness give way quickly to the record of a town growing, changing, coping with disasters, and developing a cultural, economic, and educational center for a vast area of isolated small communities north of the Alaska Range.

The first things the pictures make evident is how quickly Fairbanks developed the characteristics of a stable community with homes, shops, and services not expected in a "gold camp." The other theme that runs through the pictures is one of a basic stability and community spirit that surmounts disasters, economic booms and busts, and the weather. A quality that has been noted before but should again be mentioned is the individuality of the citizens of the area. The spectrum includes every political and social opinion available. In Fairbanks they're all evident in a vocal, active, and tolerant blend.

The pictures have come from many sources, but our greatest debt is due to the Photo Collection of the University of Alaska Archives at the Elmer E. Rasmuson Library in Fairbanks. Renee Blahuta, library assistant, was of immeasurable help with her knowledge of the materials in the collections and valuable suggestions on sources for particular photographs and topics to be illustrated. The cooperation and help of the rest of the staff of the archives was always appreciated, as was the help of the University Museum. Thanks are due also to the many people who have deposited their collections in this marvelous repository where they can be used by all. Recognition is given to these donors with the appropriate photographs. Additional thanks are due to Tillie Link and Francine Mears, Evolyn Melville, Candy Waugaman, Edith Holm, Norma Hoyt, and Helen Atkinson· Frank.

We are grateful to Kent Sturgis, managing editor of the *Fairbanks Daily News-Miner,* for giving us access to the photo collection of the newspaper. We also appreciate the cooperation of: Robert Vaughn of the Alaska Association for the Arts; Janet Baird of the Tanana Valley Fair Association; Terry Leiberman of Alaskaland; and Alaska Linck.

Many others identified locations and individuals as well as offering suggestions and encouragement.

Charles Bachus and Patricia Dyer-Smith deserve thanks for their good jobs with the photo processing and typing.

Fairbanks was a well photographed city, and these photos are a sample of the material available. Fairbanks is also a city with a band of good photographers who will continue to record the life of the town.

Introduction

Fairbanks sits at the center of the vast expanse of Interior Alaska, comprised of lowlands and rolling highlands forming the central plateau of the state. Residents have chosen to call the town "the golden heart of Alaska." On the southern horizon looms the Alaska Range, with Mount McKinley and its sister peaks visible on clear days. On the north the interior is bounded by the Brooks Range. East to west, the region extends from the Canadian boundary to the highlands about Norton Sound.

The whole area is drained by the mighty 1,979-mile-long Yukon River, third longest in North America after the Mississippi-Missouri and Mackenzie systems, and its numerous tributaries. Even in the late nineteenth century it was a land few Caucasians knew. The noted Army explorer, Henry T. Allen, had led an exceptional expedition to the interior in the 1880s. In 1886 he wrote that "it is a very remarkable fact that a region under civilized [Russian] government for more than a century should remain so completely unknown as the vast territory drained by the Copper, Tanana, and Koyukuk rivers." He should have added the Yukon River as well.

Actually, others had preceeded Allen. Over the years, a few explorers, adventurers, and prospectors had traveled up and down the Yukon River.

The Russians had established Fort Alexander at the mouth of the Nushagak River in 1818. Using it as a base for their activities, Ivan Filippovich Vasilev, Semen Lukin, and Fedor Kolmakov undertook explorations of the interior. In 1833 the Russians built Fort St. Michael north of the mouth of the Yukon River. From here, Andrei Glazunov and Vasili Malakhov explored a part of the Yukon River. In 1830 Ferdinand Petrovich Wrangell became the governor of the Russian-American colony. And although he was only in the country for a little less than five years, he showed great interest in, and encouraged, exploratory activities. During his tenure a number of important explorations took place which substantially added to the existing knowledge about Alaska's geography and Native populations. Even after his tenure as governor, Wrangell continued to encourage geographical discovery from his position as the principal director of the Russian-American Company in St. Petersburg.

The Campus Site (on the University of Alaska Campus) provides some of the earliest archeological evidence of human life in Interior Alaska. Artifacts from the site include, in the top row, a large notched pebble, a side-notched projectile point, a burin, and a microblade core. Below them are an endscraper, a projectile point, and four microblades. These tools were used by early inhabitants of the Tanana Valley and the Fairbanks area. The Campus Site was used by prehistoric people from about 10,000 B.C. to the time of the birth of Christ. Courtesy of University of Alaska Museum

Wrangell probably reacted favorably to a proposal from Lieutenant Lavrentiy A. Zagoskin, only recently transferred at his own request from the Imperial Navy to the Russian-American Company, that he be permitted to undertake extensive explorations into the interior of the vast area drained by the Yukon and Kuskokwim rivers. Zagoskin intended to gain information advantageous to the fur trade and also to consolidate and to extend the geographical discoveries made in the area in the previous twenty-five years. Between 1842 and 1844 Lieutenant Zagoskin traveled in Interior Alaska. His exploration represented the outstanding Russian achievement in Interior Alaskan exploration, and his contributions still represent a substantial and important contribution to ethnography.

Eventually, surveyors and scientists of the Collins Overland Telegraph Expedition, who planned to circle the globe with a telegraph line crossing from Alaska into Siberia, explored the

The Indians of the Interior used the waterways for travel. Beautifully constructed birch bark canoes could carry several people and their gear. Smaller boats, such as "rat canoes," were used to hunt muskrat or to reach places where portages were necessary. Courtesy of Bunnell Collection, Archives, University of Alaska, Fairbanks

Yukon Valley and planned to string a wire along the river. The project collapsed, however, when Cyrus Field successfully laid his cable across the bottom of the Atlantic Ocean.

After the purchase of Alaska in 1867, the United States Army sent several military expeditions north to determine what had been bought. Lieutenant Frederick Schwatka, an experienced Arctic explorer, led one of these expeditions in 1883. The party of six climbed over the Chilkoot Pass to the headwaters of the Yukon River and constructed a log raft at Lake Lindeman which the men christened the *Resolute.* The sturdy craft carried the party through several rapids some 1,300 miles to Nukluklayet, an old Indian trading camp and settlement on the right bank of the Yukon River near the junction of the Tanana River, and then the party abandoned the raft and went by steamer to St. Michael.

Two years after Schwatka's expedition the Army sent out another one under the command of Lieutenant Henry Allen, a West Point graduate from Kentucky. With two enlisted men and two prospectors, Allen crossed the Alaska Range to the Yukon River by ascending the Copper River and descending the Tanana River. It was an incredibly difficult journey, and Allen and his party arrived at the Yukon, and at Nukluklayet, on June 25, 1885. They were a starving, scurvy-ridden group which gratefully accepted the trader's invitation to dine on fish fried in machine oil. Allen had accomplished a remarkable feat, for nobody had ever crossed the mountains to the Yukon before. The map Allen drew after his expedition showed the Tanana River winding its way through hundreds of miles of blank space.

Chief Thomas of Nenana and his family are shown in their finest moosehide ceremonial clothing with valuable dentalium decorations. Tents were used as summer dwellings and at fish-camps in warm weather. The Indians of the Interior lived in small groups that moved to various special sites during the appropriate season to gather berries, to fish, or to hunt. Courtesy of Reuel Griffin Collection, Archives, University of Alaska, Fairbanks

A fish camp along the Tanana with a fish wheel near shore. Miners introduced the fish wheel at the beginning of the twentieth century. This device caught fish in turning baskets as they swam upstream in the silt-laden waters. Courtesy of Reuel Griffin Collection, Archives, University of Alaska, Fairbanks

Native basketmaker and family.
Photo by Johnson, Fairbanks

"Native basketmaker and family." The Indian people of the Tanana Valley lived a nomadic life dependent on the natural resources of the country. With the settlement of towns and the influx of goldminers, their way of life changed. This plate from the early 1900s shows many items such as tents, clothing, and kettles, that were bought or traded with proceeds from trapping furs, supplying meat and fish to the camps, woodcutting, or from other newly available jobs. Courtesy of Reuel Griffin Collection, Archives, University of Alaska, Fairbanks

In 1885 Lieutenant Henry Allen (middle) and two enlisted men, Private Fickett (left) and Sergeant Robertson (right), crossed the Alaska Range and descended the Tanana River to the Yukon. (Allen drew the first accurate map of the Tanana. The long, hazardous trip ended at the mouth of the Yukon.) Courtesy of Archives, University of Alaska, Fairbanks

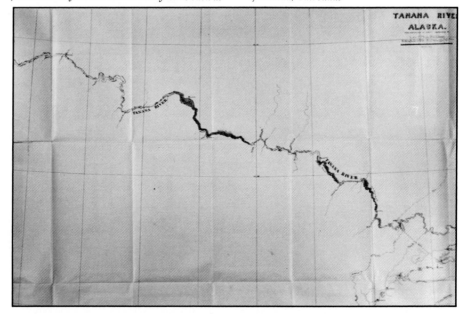

CHIEF WILLIAM OF TANANA.   PAUL WILLIAMS, TANANA.   CHIEF CHARLIE OF MINTU.
CHIEF ALEXANDER OF TOLOVANA.   CHIEF THOMAS OF NENANA.   CHIEF EVAN OF KOSCHAKAT.   CHIEF ALEXANDER WILLIAM OF TANANA.

In 1915 chiefs of the Indian villages in the Interior came to Fairbanks to meet with Judge Wickersham and to discuss their status in the developing area. In this picture they are wearing their best moosehide jackets decorated with dentalium, beads, and beaver fur. The bands of dentalium support sheaths for their knives with distinctively curved handles.

Left to right, standing: Chief William of Tanana, Paul Williams of Tanana, Chief Charlie of Mintu. Seated: Chief Alexander of Tolovana, Chief Thomas of Nenana, Chief Evan of Koschakat, Chief Alexander William of Tanana. Courtesy of Archives, University of Alaska, Fairbanks

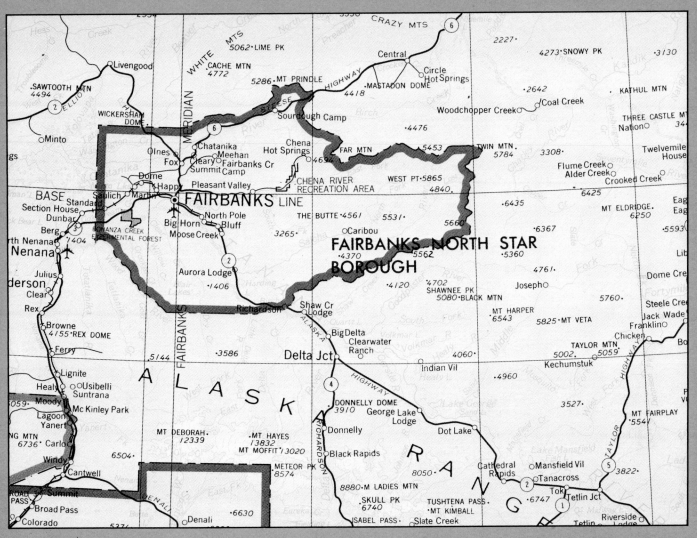

Fairbanks, "the golden heart of Alaska," serves as a service and distribution center for the great area north of the Alaska Range. The little towns just north of Fairbanks made up a major mining district. United States Geological Survey map

The Lavelle Young, *a steamer chartered by E. T. Barnette after his own boat, the* Arctic Boy, *was wrecked, had brought Barnette as far as it could up the Tanana and Chena rivers. At about four o'clock in the afternoon on August 26, 1901, the* Lavelle Young *tied up to a high wooden bank and unloaded Barnette's goods. The steamer made other trips up the Yukon and Tanana to the new town. This is probably 1904. Courtesy of Archives, University of Alaska, Fairbanks*

Chapter I

GOLD RUSH TOWN

1902-1913

Even before Schwatka's and Allen's expeditions, American traders had taken over the scattered Russian and English trading posts in the Yukon Valley. By the early 1870s prospectors already were exploring the upper reaches of the river, and in the fall of 1886, Howard Franklin struck placer gold on Franklin Creek, a tributary of the Forty-Mile River, which flows into the Yukon. This was the first strike in American territory because all gold before this had been found on sandbars along the Canadian stretch of the Yukon River. Prospectors soon stampeded to the region and found gold in a wide area in rich bedrock deposits straddling the American-Canadian border. Paydirt was found on Chicken Creek, Miller Creek, Franklin Gulch, and other tributaries of the Forty-Mile River. Miners established a settlement approximately twenty five miles from the American border, some thirty-four miles downriver from Fort Reliance, the trading and supply post on the upper Yukon operated by Jack McQuesten, Arthur Harper, and Alfred Mayo since 1874. The discovery of gold in the Forty Mile region accelerated the pace of events on the Yukon River.

By 1893 prospectors had found gold on Birch Creek, 240 miles downriver from Forty Mile. This discovery led to the founding of Circle. By 1895 Circle far surpassed Forty Mile in population.

Late in the fall of 1896, miners at Circle and Forty Mile heard that George Washington Carmack and his two Indian companions, Skookum Jim and Tagish Charley, had found gold in the Canadian Klondike in quantities never before seen in the Yukon country. Carmack staked his first claim on August 17, 1896, in the region that soon was to become world famous. By early winter most of the men from Forty Mile had rushed to the Klondike and staked claims.

Circle was farther away, and the first rumors about the new strike were not believed until January 1897, when Arthur Walden rushed into town with

In 1901 Felix Pedro (shown here) was working in the hills above the Tanana Valley with his partner, Tom Gilmore. In August, when in need of supplies, he saw the Lavelle Young in the Chena over twenty miles away. After getting more supplies, they continued their search for gold. When Pedro struck gold in July of 1902, the future of Fairbanks, Barnette's trading post, was assured. Courtesy of Archives, University of Alaska, Fairbanks

letters for saloon keeper Harry Ash. The saloon keeper's partner had hit it big and summoned Ash to join him. Within hours, virtually everyone in Circle rushed to the Klondike.

The Klondike discovery spurred men to search the North for gold. In 1898 gold was discovered on Anvil Creek, a short tributary of the Snake River on the Seward Peninsula, and by 1899 thousands of miners stampeded to this American Klondike.

By 1901 several prospectors were searching the Tanana Valley and found excellent placer prospects. Some years earlier, Felix Pedro, an Italian-American, had discovered gold along one of the then-unnamed tributaries of the Tanana River. He marked the spot and went to Circle to obtain supplies. Once re-supplied, he returned but, to his dismay, could not locate his discovery. Yet he did not give up, and finally he and his partner, Tom Gilmore, found several potentially rich gold deposits along Fish Creek and Gold Stream.

In the meantime, Captain E. T. Barnette, who soon was to play a leading role in the development of the Tanana Valley, found himself stranded at St. Michael in July 1901 with some 125 tons of trade goods on hand. He had planned to take his load on his boat, the *Arctic Boy,* to the Valdez-Eagle crossing, some 400 miles up the Tanana River above Fort Weare, where he wanted to establish a trading post, but his boat had just been wrecked on the rocks in St. Michael Harbor. Barnette knew many people, for he

was no stranger to the North. As early as 1897 he had taken a boatload of trading goods up the Yukon River to Dawson and apparently made a good profit. Now in his need, Barnette turned to Captain C. W. Adams and persuaded him to lease the *Lavelle Young* to him.

On August 8, 1901, the 150-foot long boat with a beam of thirty four feet was fully loaded with freight. Accompanying Barnette were his wife, four other men, a horse, and a dog team. Working its way up the Yukon, the boat burned approximately one cord of wood per day. At Fort Weare, Adams picked up two pilots who were to assist him in navigating the tricky Tanana River.

The *Lavelle Young* finally reached the mouth of the Chena River, where Hendricks and Belt maintained a trading post. The boat turned into the river and traveled about seven miles before it branched into several channels, all of them too shallow for the *Lavelle Young's* four-foot draft. Captain Adams soon decided that it was impossible to go any farther. He called Barnette to the pilot house and told him that he had "guaranteed to take you as far as the boat would go up the Tanana. I can't cross mountains with it."

Barnette clearly was unhappy. He told the captain that he had talked to an Indian who knew how to get through the Chena River and back to the Tanana River. The men discussed the situation further, and Adams finally tried one more time to go

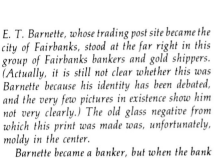

E. T. Barnette, whose trading post site became the city of Fairbanks, stood at the far right in this group of Fairbanks bankers and gold shippers. (Actually, it is still not clear whether this was Barnette because his identity has been debated, and the very few pictures in existence show him not very clearly.) The old glass negative from which this print was made was, unfortunately, moldy in the center.

Barnette became a banker, but when the bank failed, he left town under a cloud. Only the names of a street and a school remain to remind Fairbanksans of their founder. Courtesy of Mary Whalen Collection; Archives, University of Alaska, Fairbanks

on. He ran out of water. Barnette thereupon demanded to be taken back to the mouth of the Chena River, but Adams refused because it was very difficult to get off a sandbar going downstream. The captain stated that "often, before you know it you're hard aground with the current holding you there. It can delay you for days," especially since the *Lavelle Young* had no steam winch or steam capstan. Adams and Barnette finally spotted a high, timbered bank and unloaded there.

Meanwhile, up in the hills, Pedro and Gilmore were about to return to Circle for supplies when the two men spotted smoke on the horizon. Standing on a hill overlooking the valley, later named Pedro Dome, they watched a small steamboat slowly move up the Chena River and dock along the bank. The two men took three days to get to the Chena River where they had seen the steamboat. They discovered that it was the *Lavelle Young.* Pedro and Gilmore then stocked up on beans, flour, and bacon and showed the crew some gold samples they had taken from a nearby stream.

The meeting between Pedro and Barnette on that fall day in 1901 established the location of the future town of Fairbanks on the Chena River, about five miles above its junction with the Tanana. Barnette thus became the founding father of Fairbanks.

But it was a meeting between Barnette and federal Judge James Wickersham at St. Michael

which resulted in Barnette's trading post being named "Fairbanks." Wickersham, who had established his headquarters at Eagle for the Third Judicial District, discovered in talking with Barnette that the two had mutual interests. They soon reached an understanding: Barnette would name his post "Fairbanks" in honor of Republican Senator Charles W. Fairbanks of Indiana, while, for his part, Wickersham would see to it that Barnette succeeded in his ventures. As Barnette put it: "If we should ever want aid at the National Capitol we would have the friendship of someone who could help us."

By 1903 a rush was on to Fairbanks, and perhaps as many as 1,000 stampeders arrived. That March, Judge Wickersham visited Fairbanks and decided to transfer his judicial headquarters from Eagle to the new town—which gave Fairbanks a significant boost in prestige and political stature. By 1904 Fairbanks had grown into a sizable settlement with a population of 3,000 and gold production of $350,000; in 1905 the population had doubled to 6,000 and gold production reached $3,750,000. In 1906, with a population of 8,000, the gold output was $9,175,000.

With great demand for lumber and abundant spruce forests nearby, entrepreneurs quickly established sawmills. The finished wood was used in buildings, and in 1905 the sawmills turned out railroad ties in great numbers. A railroad was not far behind, and on July 17, 1905, Fairbanks residents celebrated the completion of the first fourteen-mile division of the line, first called the Tanana Mines Railroad and later renamed the Tanana Valley Railroad. Eventually, the thirty-four-mile narrow-gauge mining road connected Chena, at the head of steamboat navigation on the Tanana, with various mining camps in the Fairbanks district, ending at Chatanika, a gold rush settlement on the river of the same name. A spur line ran 4.7 miles northeast to Fairbanks as well.

In April 1906 disaster befell the young town. A three-story building on the corner of First and Cushman caught fire and burned rapidly. A cupola on top of the building fell and broke the fire hydrant on the corner, causing the water to escape from the

inadequate to fight a major conflagration. Their equipment had consisted of a few buckets, ladders, and fire axes and several water holes in the river which volunteers were expected to keep open during the winter.

After the disastrous 1906 fire, the city established a paid fire department. After three years the city pronounced the department an unqualified success, for it had suffered property losses from fire amounting to $12,596, or less than one-sixth of one percent of evaluation. The cost of running the department had amounted to $90,000. In the three years, the department had responded to 166 alarms. The average property loss for each one came to $178.50. In 1909, J. J. Buckley was the chief, H. J.

The corner of First Avenue and Cushman Street in 1903. The Fairbanks—a bar and hotel—continued later in more modern quarters. Courtesy of Archives, University of Alaska, Fairbanks

main and the pressure in all other hydrants to drop. There was little water to use against the fire, and despite the frantic efforts of the power plant, burning wood, kerosene, lard, and bacon, water pressure remained totally inadequate. The fire rapidly spread and virtually destroyed the town's central area. Fortunately, the fire occurred in the spring and thus lessened the hardships on those dispossessed. Rebuilding started immediately, and Fairbanks citizens were optimistic. Businessmen put up signs announcing "a genuine fire sale" and built new quarters.

The Northern Commercial Company alleviated fears of shortages with an ad in the newspaper the day after the fire that there were enough supplies in town for everybody and that prices would not be raised. The popular Fraction Bar had been burned out, but the next day it was in business again, advertising "fresh bar, fresh air, and good treatment." Within a month most of the devastated area had been rebuilt. This effort reflected well on the energy of Fairbanks residents, but also told much about the quality of the buildings.

Fairbanks citizens had learned from the devastating fire and realized that the volunteer fire department, organized in the summer of 1903, was

Gohres the captain, and William Roberts, Adolph Olsen, Jack O'Connor, and H. A. King served as firemen. The team boasted of one hose wagon and team with 5,000 feet of 2½ inch rubber-lined hose. In addition, there was a chemical engine with a capacity of 100 gallons.

By 1908 Fairbanks had a population of 3,500, with another 15,000 in the district, and the gold output reached $9,250,000 despite some labor problems. Transporting goods to Fairbanks was a most critical need. In the first couple of years, the overland trail from Circle City on the Yukon sufficed, with its roadhouses spaced at twenty-mile intervals, to care for the needs of the travelers. But as the population of the Tanana Valley increased, this route became inadequate.

The climate dictated the transportation routes. During the ice-free summer months sternwheel steamers, built to draw less water than most of the Yukon River boats, carried freight and passengers on the Tanana and Chena rivers. These shallower draft boats connected with the Yukon steamers at Tanana and at the Army post of Fort Gibbon, located where the Tanana joined the Yukon some 235 miles below Fairbanks. This river route gave access to the Out-

This early view, before breakup in 1903, shows a few cabins in the wilderness at what would become Second Avenue and Cushman Street. The tent with a faint sign in the center of the photo was a laundry. Courtesy of Archives, University of Alaska, Fairbanks

The corner of Third Avenue and Cushman Street, looking west in 1903. Cabins are being built and the forest is receding. Courtesy of Archives, University of Alaska, Fairbanks

side via connections at St. Michael at the Yukon's mouth and Dawson near its upper reaches.

Summers were short, however, and an overland connection had to be developed to supply the town and its surrounding mining camps during the remainder of the year. And since the various gold discoveries had focused congressional attention on Alaska, the United States Senate appointed a subcommittee of its Committee on Territories to journey to Alaska in 1903 and make a "thorough investigation of existing conditions, her resources and her needs, with the purpose to ascertain and report what, if any, legislation is required for that district." The four senators traveled extensively and held hearings at scattered locations. Witnesses repeatedly asked that the government build wagon roads from points along the Yukon to the mining camps. On their return, the subcommittee recommended that the government construct a system of transporta-

tion routes.

Congress soon established a Board of Road Commissioners for Alaska, and the president signed the legislation in 1905. By 1906 the board devoted considerable attention and effort to constructing a wagon road between Valdez and Fairbanks. From the ice-free port of Valdez, the crude trail threaded Keystone Canyon on the Lowe River, and in eighteen miles climbed 3,000 feet through the Chugach Range to Thompson Pass. From there it skirted the Copper River, descended to Paxson and Summit lakes, rising abruptly again to 3,000 foot Isabel Pass through the Alaska Range and reaching the Big Delta and Tanana rivers. After some 367 miles the trail reached Fairbanks.

At first only dog teams traveled the trail, but it was not long until improvements by the board enabled horse-drawn double enders and stages to operate on a regular schedule, departing both Valdez

Valdez was a gateway to the new gold strike at Fairbanks. Part of the route had been tried before on the way to the Klondike. Here, stampeders head up the horseshoe on the way to the summit.

Horse-drawn sled and dog teams were usually used, but the last man in the line is pushing his faithful bicycle. Courtesy of Bunnell Collection, Archives, University of Alaska, Fairbanks

Volume I, Number 1 of The Fairbanks Gazette *came out on July 17, 1903. It was one of the first papers in the camp, and the lead article defended discoveries. Courtesy of Archives, University of Alaska, Fairbanks*

and Fairbanks at ten-day intervals. The stages carried the U. S. mail, passengers, and Wells Fargo express. Some twenty five roadhouses along the trail provided comfort and rest for travelers and horses alike. Many walked the trail on foot, and some of the more adventurous even used bicycles.

Fairbanks was not as isolated as many imagined it to be, however. The Army constructed the extensive Washington-Alaska Cable and Telegraph System or WAMCATS, as it was called. It finished the 1,506 miles of overland lines and a few hundred miles of submarine cable in 1903. Thereafter, except for interruptions caused by winter storms and summer floods and forest fires, Fairbanks citizens received the world's daily news as speedily as Seattle or San Francisco.

While Chena declined, Fairbanks prospered, particularly after Judge Wickersham had moved his court to town. By 1907 the town had a bookstore, two hospitals (St. Joseph's and St. Matthew's), a greenhouse, and two fortune tellers, Mmes. Melbourne and Zelpha. Readers of Fairbanks newspapers in 1908 learned that the little railroad would handle livestock only by special arrangements, but would carry empty beer kegs and soda bottles free; that ice and roller rinks and moving pictures advertised for customers; that rentals were scarce and that many desired to buy cabins. There were Sunday concerts featuring such original compositions as a "Toast to the Brides of Fairbanks" and the "Fairbanks Tickle," and feature writers commented on the increasing use of cigarettes. The grocery department of the Northern Commercial Company advertised pate de foie gras, crab meat, Russian caviar, and imported anchovies.

In short, Fairbanks had quickly become a town of homes, families, and children, offering many of life's amenities. Its people represented many nationalities, such as Slavonians, Italians, Scots, Japanese, Swedes, and Norwegians; its residents came from nearly every state of the Union, and from every social stratum and occupation.

Fairbanks quickly became the center of social, economic, and political development in the Tanana Valley, but it was not the only community which developed. Within an approximate radius of thirty miles, more than twenty separate mining communities sprang up and prospered for varying lengths of time before declining and disappearing. The most important of these were:

• Alder Creek Camp, on the left bank of Fairbanks Creek, 21 miles northeast of Fairbanks.

• Berry (Ester), trail junction 1 mile east of Ester, 8 miles west of Fairbanks, named for the Berry brothers in 1906.

• Cleary City (Gates City), established in 1904, some 24 miles northeast of Fairbanks. At its height, Cleary had 17 saloons, electric lights, telephone service, a jail, a volunteer fire company, a courthouse, and 2 hospitals, 3 banks, a church, stores, a school, and a lumber yard. It was the supply and banking center for the region northeast of Fairbanks with a population of approximately 2,000.

• Dome City, located on Dome Creek, 16 miles northeast of Fairbanks, founded in 1906. In 1908 it had a population of 800 and had hotels, electric lights, telephone service, banking facilities, a hospi-

If you couldn't afford a horse or dog team, there was little alternative to pulling the load yourself. The caption reads '"By the Neck' to Fairbanks," over 360 miles on a trail that was cold and stormy in the winter and crossed swift streams and rivers and muddy ground in summer. The roadhouses that sprang up along it were a welcome relief for tired travelers. Courtesy of Bunnell Collection, Archives, University of Alaska, Fairbanks

tal, and daily stage service to Fox, the nearest station on the railroad.

• Eldorado City on Eldorado Creek, a tributary of the Chatanika River, 24 miles north of Fairbanks and 4 miles north of Dome City. The camp had a post office and twice-weekly mail service, 2 roadhouses, a store, and a saloon. In 1906 it had a population of approximately 75.

• Engineer Creek Camp, located 20 miles north of Fairbanks on Engineer Creek, some 11 miles north of Fox. It had a post office and was active into the 1950s. Miners had established the camp in 1909.

• Ester City (Berry), founded in 1905-1906, had several stores, a post office, and the California Hotel. In 1965 the name was changed to honor Ester Duffy of the California Hotel.

• Fox, founded in 1904, is located 10 miles northeast of Fairbanks. In 1907 it had a population of 500 and a reputation as a wide open, rowdy mining camp with a string of bawdy houses. It had a post office from 1907 to 1948, 2 hotels, 2 restaurants, a bakery, a laundry, 2 general stores, a flume hose factory, telephone service, and twice-weekly mail delivery.

• Gilmore, located 11 miles northeast of Fairbanks, on the right bank of Pedro Creek. Established in 1904-1905, it was the railroad terminus until construction of the Chatanika spur.

• Golden City, located at the junction of Pedro and Twin creeks, 18 miles northeast of Fairbanks, was founded in 1903.

• Olnes, 25 miles north of Fairbanks and 15 miles below Dome Creek. Established in 1904-1905 as a railroad station, it apparently had over 30 buildings, a post office, daily mail delivery, telephone facilities, and stage service to Tolovana, 53 miles to the west.

• Vault, located 12 miles north of Fairbanks, established in 1905-1906, had a population of approximately 200 and 2 roadhouses, 3 stores, 3 saloons, and 9 mining operations.

With the exception of a few old-timers and seasonal miners, these communities have long been abandoned with the exception of Fox which has developed into a thriving little community.

The residents of Fairbanks clearly were enterprising people. As early as the summer of 1903 they had incorporated the town in order to regulate municipal affairs. In the fall of that year the first school opened with one teacher and thirteen students. Funds, however, ran out and the school closed during the winter. In 1904 the town built a small schoolhouse, and in the fall fifty students applied for admission, representing all grades from the first to high school. An influx of many families in the late fall forced the town fathers to rent the Masonic Hall for additional space. By 1906 growing enrollments had necessitated numerous expansions to the original school, and in that year the first high school class, consisting of ten freshmen students, enrolled.

Chena grew up as a rival to Fairbanks. Located just below the mouth of the Chena River on the Tanana River, it was an easier stop for steamers than the Chena River at Fairbanks. The Tanana Valley Railroad had its main terminal here. The decision by Judge James Wickersham to locate his federal court in Fairbanks and the high price of city lots eventually led to the decline of Chena. Many of the buildings were moved to Nenana during the construction of the Alaska Railroad. The river has cut away much of the bank, and all of the once busy community is gone. Courtesy of Laura M. Hills Collection, Archives, University of Alaska, Fairbanks

Fairbanks Alaska July 4th 1904

At the end of 1907 the city council had provided for the construction of a new school.

The school board provided free textbooks as well as supplementary readers to the students. A number of public-spirited citizens soon organized a benefit concert and used the $400 in profits to acquire some 350 volumes which became the foundation of the school library.

Approximately 150 students attended the Fairbanks Public School in 1907 and all but 17 were enrolled in the grade school. While the academic courses had been well organized by 1907, little had been done to establish a program of school athletics. The high school girls, however, had formed a basketball team and played several of the town's ladies' teams, while the high school boys joined forces with a few of the young men not attending school and played one of the town's fraternal organizations.

In the meantime, citizens had established several other schools in the Tanana Valley. One was located on the opposite side of the slough from Fairbanks serving the two small communities of Garden Island and Graehl. It had opened its door in September 1908, enrolling twelve students. About eight miles below Fairbanks, where the Chena River emptied into the Tanana, lay the little town of Chena. Incorporated in 1903, it was principally a settlement of warehouses and served as a supply point for Fairbanks and the creeks where miners dug the gold. Chena had maintained a public school from its founding, but its enrollment had been modest. Efforts had also been made to build schools on the many creeks surrounding Fairbanks. The school at Cleary, north of Fairbanks, had been the most successful, averaging an enrollment of twelve children.

Edby Davis was one young scholar who arrived in Fairbanks in 1906 at the age of eleven together with his family. He recalled those early Fairbanks days years later. School days were busy ones, but

July 4, 1904, saw a community spreading along the banks of the Chena. An early version of the temporary wooden bridge is in place. A remaining structure is the Northern Commercial Company building on the far right, which is now incorporated into the Nordstrom store building. Courtesy of Bunnell Collection, Archives, University of Alaska, Fairbanks

eventually the summer arrived and brought with it free time and warm weather. Davis related that the boys often walked to the second slough on the railway, a favorite swimming hole. They would leave the Turner Street bridge armed with a smudge pot to ward off the ferocious mosquitoes. The pot was a lard pail with holes in the bottom and filled with decayed wood, grass, and anything else producing a heavy smoke. Once at the swimming hole, the boys undressed and dived into the water in the raw. After their swim, they would rush to the smudge pot, dry themselves, get dressed, and then ignite small smudges and walk home.

The Fourth of July was a time for celebrating in Fairbanks. The town folks erected a grandstand on First Avenue between Cushman Street and the Fairview Hotel. Special trains carried miners at reduced rates from the outlying creeks to town. On the morning of the Fourth a clergyman mounted a platform supported by beer kegs and gave the invocation. Other speakers talked about the founding fathers and the American Revolution, and then came the races. After each one the band played, and all adults rushed into the numerous saloons to slake their thirst. Saloons and eating establishments were crowded all day. Visitors and residents thoroughly enjoyed the holiday.

During these early years, Edby Davis earned spending money selling the *Fairbanks News* on the streets, receiving twenty five cents for the four-page paper and retaining approximately half of that sum as profit. And although there were to be scores of short-lived newspapers in the Tanana Valley, it was the *Fairbanks News,* which George M. Hill had established as early as 1903, that survived and eventually became the *Fairbanks Daily News-Miners* of today.

By 1909 fortunes had been won and lost in the gold mining business in the Fairbanks region. The town also boasted of numerous prominent citizen entrepreneurs. One of these was Judge J. C. Kellum. Born in Jackson County, Missouri, he graduated from Harvard University in 1873 and subsequently practiced law in Kansas City, Missouri. He then moved to Arizona in 1887, and then went to Dawson in 1898. While there, he was associated with the town's leading law firm, Wade, Clark & Wilson. Restless, he moved to Circle on the Yukon in 1909 and finally took up his residence in Fairbanks in the winter of 1902-1903. He quickly became a member of the law firm of Claypool, Kellum & Cowles as partner. A man of means, Kellum had substantial holdings in various leading Fairbanks enterprises, such as the Tanana Bottling Works, the Tanana Valley Railroad, and the Tanana Electric Company. He also had substantial real estate holdings and became one of the pioneer mining men as well. Probably his richest claim was No. 6 below on the right bank of Cleary Creek. (Mining claims are

A crowd watches the transfer of a gold shipment at the Washington-Alaska bank. The consolidated Fairbanks Banking Company/Washington Alaska Bank had E. T. Barnette as president. After his resignation and departure, the bank

numbered from the discovery claim. Hence No. 6 below means that the property was located six claims below the discovery claim.) Between 1905 and 1907 the miners who had leased his claim and were called lay men recovered some $40,000 worth of gold in a nine-day sluicing operation alone.

John Ronan was a Kansas farm boy who left his home at the age of twenty one in 1891 to seek his fortune in the hills and plains of Nebraska, Iowa, the Dakotas, Montana, and Washington. Hearing of the Klondike strike in 1898, he went north. After much moving about, he finally went to Fairbanks. Together with his partner, Matt Matheson, he purchased interests in various claims on Cleary Creek and made much money. Interested in politics, he ran unsuc-

collapsed in 1911. The man in the white shirt in front of the door appears to be Felix Pedro. Courtesy of Bunnell Collection, Archives, University of Alaska, Fairbanks

cessfully as a Democrat for the position of delegate to Congress and then returned to mining on Cleary, Chatanika, Fairbanks, and Engineer creeks.

G. T. Ervin hailed from Georgia and arrived in Fairbanks in early 1904 from Dawson, where he had successfully mined. Shortly after his arrival he was elected city magistrate, an office which he held for two terms and which brought him the appellation "Judge." The Judge soon became one of the largest dealers in firewood, which his teams delivered in four-foot lengths to residences as well as to the Northern Commercial Company boilers. Judge Erwin also had mining interests and owned half of the firm of Heimburger & Company, which operated on Ester Creek.

A. J. Nordale made his living as a hotel man. He came to Alaska in 1896 and settled in Juneau. In 1897 he left that city and went to Dawson, Yukon Territory, where he remained until 1904, all the time engaging in the hotel and restaurant business. In 1904 Nordale went to Cleary City, north of Fairbanks, where he operated the Grand Hotel until 1908, when he moved to Fairbanks and became the proprietor of the Nordale Hotel on First Avenue on the site of the old Riverside Hotel, which had been destroyed in the 1906 fire.

H. Markley Badger was born in Minnesota in 1869, went to California in 1889, and to Washington in 1890, where he farmed in the Skagit Valley for ten years. In January 1900 he left for Dawson via Skagway. It took him forty days to reach his destination, dragging his sled loaded with supplies and living in a tent with the thermometer sometimes dropping to sixty-five degrees below zero. Badger mined three years on Bonanza Creek and hearing of the strike in the Tanana Valley left Dawson and arrived in Fairbanks in March 1903. He presided over the first miner's meeting held in the Tanana, where the angry men considered taking Barnette's trading post by force and distributing sorely needed supplies. Cool judgment prevailed, however, and the miners reached a settlement with the canny trader. In 1904, after gold production began, Badger opened the first real estate office in the valley, and Fairbanks citizens elected him to the position of town recorder. Business increased so rapidly that Badger took in a partner in 1907. The new firm was called Badger & Woodward, Brokers.

C. S. Sargent was another businessman. A native of Massachusetts, he came to Skagway in 1897 and arrived in Dawson the following year. There, together with his partner, he organized the firm of Sargent & Pinska in February, 1899. The firm quickly became one of the leading mercantile institutions in the Yukon metropolis. With the decline of Dawson, he established a store in Fairbanks on June 1, 1904. The big 1906 fire destroyed both their store and warehouse, but undeterred, the partners immediately rebuilt.

A growing community like Fairbanks had a voracious appetite for construction materials, particularly lumber. Roy Rutherford and Sylvestor Widman recognized the opportunities, and in September 1906 established the Independent Lumber Company. They built a large saw and plane mill along the Chena River near the wireless station. Lumberjacks cut the necessary logs on the upper Chena River and floated them to the mill. The business grew so rapidly that the two men soon had to open a downtown office on the city dock. Independent Lumber Company, after numerous reorganizations, still does business in Fairbanks in 1981.

Fairbanks also offered opportunities for many

An early scene at one of the creeks about 1910. The man at the left is turning a windlass to raise gold-bearing gravel from the shaft. Courtesy of Bunnell Collection, Archives, University of Alaska, Fairbanks

The original caption reads "The largest shipment of machinery leaving Fairbanks for the creeks to date, July 21, 1904." The three large wagon loads include a boiler on the first wagon. The Alaska Machinery Company is still housed in a tent at this early date. The roads to the mining operations were still pretty rough, but Fairbanks was recognized as the supply center. Electric power poles appear behind the buildings under construction in the still-forested townsite. Courtesy of Norma Hoyt Collection

lawyers, among them Natalie Roberts Moore, wife of Dr. C. M. Moore, a dentist. Mrs. Moore came from Massachusetts, moved with her family to Tacoma, finished high school, and attended the Annie Wright Seminary for Girls. She then studied law with a Tacoma firm and was admitted to practice before the Supreme Court at Olympia, Washington, in October 1899. She came to Fairbanks in 1905, where she met and married Dr. Moore and was admitted to practice law in Alaska in 1908.

In short, by 1910 the Tanana Valley was home to a varied group of individuals with many skills. In that year, the valley held an estimated population of 11,000 while Fairbanks had 3,541. Gold production in 1909 had amounted to about $10.5 million, while the value of merchandise shipped from the States to Fairbanks amounted to $2,305,993. In addition to St. Joseph's Hospital, the Episcopal Church had built St. Mathew's Hospital, located between the church and the rectory. For a small frontier community Fairbanks had an astounding variety of businesses by 1910. The B, H & K Foundry and Shops constructed most any piece of machinery used in the valley, on steamboats and in mining operations. A forty horse-power boiler furnished the plant with steam, located in a 100-foot by 150-foot building. The Tanana Valley Railroad ran a spur track directly into the warehouse. The plant employed fourteen men on a year-round basis.

At the lower end of town the Northern Navigation Company maintained a large shipyard which enabled necessary repairs to be carried out on riverboats not exceeding 150 feet in length. New vessels were built as well, and in the spring, just before the opening of the navigation season when boats were readied for the summer's work, the yard employed as many as 100 men with a daily payroll of $752.

Across the river from Fairbanks, in Graehl, Sam Jensen was the proprietor of a complete shipbuilding plant for the construction of motorboats and all manner of smaller river craft, such as poling and rowboats. In the spring of 1910 Jensen had built a motor launch for Charles E. Freeman of Fairbanks. Christened the *Emmaline,* the craft was twenty-eight feet in length, narrow and trim, with a four-and-a-half foot beam, powered by a six horse-power, two cylinder engine. Designed both as a pleasure craft or freighter, it seated sixteen people comfortably, consuming seven and one-half gallons of gasoline for a ten-hour run at full speed.

Fairbanksans were a thirsty group, and the Barthel Brewing Company, located at the west end of town, slaked the thirst. Proud citizens maintained that the plant "is one which would hold its own in point of equipment and capacity with those located on the Outside in cities of ten times its size. Furthermore, the excellent water used and the capable brewers employed produced a product 'the equal of that made in any part of the country.'" The main building of the brewery was four stories high with two cellars each 15 feet high. The brewery had a storage capacity of 150 tons besides the hot and cold water tanks, and the icehouse, six feet underground, held 300 tons of ice. The brewhouse had a capacity of 100 barrels a day, and the bottling department was capable of bottling 30 barrels a day, enough to furnish every resident of the camp with about one bottle per day. The proprietor was Herman Barthel, who had learned the skill in his native Prussia.

The area from First and Turner to First and Lacey was called the Great White Way and consisted mostly of saloons and gambling establishments. The City Hall and Fire Department were located on Third and Turner and dead-ended the street. The Flora-dora, a combination saloon and dance hall, was

The Orr Stage Line to Valdez is on its way with supplies, hay for the horses, and a passenger, Eddie E. M. Wilson, has a large sign up boasting "I am going OUT 2 B Married." Although there were many families in Fairbanks, men still outnumbered women. Courtesy of Bunnell Collection, Archives, University of Alaska, Fairbanks

located on Fourth and Cushman, but a court order soon closed it. Across Fourth and Cushman and Barnette, enclosed by a high board fence, was the red light district, an area closed down in the 1940s.

It is apparent that by 1910 Fairbanks had grown into a bustling little frontier town which offered its citizens many of the amenities usually found only in larger towns, including telephone and telegraph services, electricity, and steam heat. Soon the first automobiles also appeared, fueled by gasoline shipped in wooden cases with two five gallon cans per case. Each gallon cost eighty cents, a price which did not change until 1923 when the Alaska Railroad, just completed, shipped gasoline in 10,000 gallon tanks. Then the price per gallon dropped to forty cents.

By 1910, however, new gold discoveries had become rare and the population started to dwindle. For the first time there was a considerable drop in gold production, from $10.5 million in 1909 to $6.1 million. This decline continued until 1915. In 1911 production amounted to $4.5 million, in 1912 $4.15 million, some $3.3 million in 1913, and $2.5 million in

1914. In 1915 production increased slightly to $3.0 million.

Fairbanks citizens quickly claimed that the decline in gold production was chargeable to the prevailing economic conditions nationally and not to the exhaustion of the gold deposits. It was true, however, that the easily mined shallow gravels had been depleted. In order to thaw the frozen ground, miners had practically denuded the readily accessible timber, and wood prices increased rapidly, adding to the cost of production. By far the greatest remaining deposits were buried under eighty to ninety feet of thick, frozen overburden. To reach this gold, operators needed fuel to thaw the ground, more powerful hoisting and thawing equipment, and other machinery as well, a process which required large capital outlays. The high cost of operating such equipment together with inadequate transportation greatly hindered the development of modern mining methods. And even though the Board of Road Commissioners for Alaska finished the crude wagon road from Valdez to Fairbanks, the decline continued.

"The Invincible Prospector." Small claims that could be worked by just a few men were usual at the beginning of gold mining in the Fairbanks area. The man in the foreground is using a rocker to separate the gold from the gravel, the one behind uses a windlass to bring up gravel from a shaft. A steam boiler is behind him, used to thaw the frozen ground. Courtesy of Bunnell Collection, Archives, University of Alaska, Fairbanks

"The 750,000 Gold Train leaving Fairbanks for the Outside over the Winter Trail, Nov. 19th, 1907." It was a cold day by the look of the ice fog and the breath of the horses, but not too cold for hats and caps on the men instead of snugger headgear. Fairbanks was a wood-burning town before the railroad was completed and coal became available. Low-lying smoke and resultant ice fog were common in early Fairbanks. Courtesy of Helen L. Atkinson Collection

SHIPMENT OF ONE AND ONE HALF TONS FAIRBANKS GOLD LEAVING VALDEZ ALASKA. CANTWELL

Valdez was the logical port for shipments to and from Fairbanks. Many supplies were brought in after Major Wilds P. Richardson completed the wagon trail in 1909. Here a shipment of one and one-half tons of Fairbanks gold is shipped to Seattle on the steamer *Saratoga*. *Courtesy of Bunnell Collection, Archives, University of Alaska, Fairbanks*

Anna and George La Montagne posed proudly with their daughter, Margaret. Anna's sister is at the left. The La Montagnes mined for many years in the Goldstream area. *Courtesy of Margaret Lentz Collection, Archives, University of Alaska, Fairbanks*

Chatanika was a thriving town for a few years before World War I. This well-dressed crowd posed on July 4, 1910, at midnight. Courtesy of Margaret Lentz Collection, Archives, University of Alaska, Fairbanks

The Union Mining Company crew at 17 Goldstream. Anna La Montagne is in the center of the group of men. Her husband, George, is to her right (in a light-colored shirt). Courtesy of Margaret Lentz Collection, Archives, University of Alaska, Fairbanks

The interior of the cook house at the Hendrickson and Johnson mine at 10 below, Cleary Creek, about 1910. Cleary Creek and the town of Cleary were named for E. T. Barnette's brother-in-law, who stayed at the trading post on the Chena the first winter, 1901. Courtesy of Margaret Lentz Collection, Archives, University of Alaska, Fairbanks

The Tanana Mines Railroad at Chena—a view of the station and the warehouses near the Tanana River. The name was changed to Tanana Valley Railroad, and eventually the line was purchased and incorporated into the Alaska Railroad while the lines to the mining camps were abandoned. These views are in 1905. Courtesy of Falcon Joslin Collection, Archives, University of Alaska, Fairbanks

The Tanana Valley Railroad at Fox Station (about eleven miles now by road) from Fairbanks. The bustling mining camp that almost completely vanished is now growing again as a stop on the road to the north. Courtesy of Falcon Joslin Collection, Archives, University of Alaska, Fairbanks

The Tanana Mines Railroad was later called the Tanana Valley Railroad. It ran from Chena to the towns in the Cleary and Chatanika areas with a spur to Fairbanks.

The Loop Roadhouse in the Goldstream area, photographed June 29, 1910, was run by Henry Baatz, according to the sign. The doorway on the left was labeled the "Ladies Entrance" and the door on the right "Bar." Courtesy of Margaret Lentz Collection, Archives, University of Alaska, Fairbanks

The small engines of the Tanana Valley Railroad burned wood, and a constant supply was needed along the line. Courtesy of Falcon Joslin Collection, Archives, University of Alaska, Fairbanks

Gilmore was a small mining camp just north of Fairbanks and a stop on the Tanana Valley Railroad. The roadhouse, a small store, and a railway station provided services for the hardworking miners. Courtesy of Archives, University of Alaska, Fairbanks

The Fairbanks waterfront was busy with steamer traffic coming from both Dawson and St. Michael until the Alaska Railroad came through in 1925. The Pioneer Dock and the Northern Commercial (N. C.) Company dock were just below the present Cushman Street Bridge. Courtesy of Archives, University of Alaska, Fairbanks

Very early in its history, Fairbanks developed good medical services. When Mrs. D. Jones persuaded her husband, in 1906, to donate $500 toward the construction of a hospital, several friends followed suit and then handed the subscription list to Father Monroe of the Catholic Church and asked him to start a hospital. At first there seemed to be no difficulties in raising the remaining funds, but the great fire of May 22, 1906, all but destroyed the town, seemingly dooming the hospital. At this point the Reverend R. J. Crimont, Prefect Apostolic of the Catholic Church in Alaska, came to the aid of the project by negotiating various loans amounting to $25,000. Thereupon the Catholic Church built the three-story St. Joseph's Hospital which opened on Thanksgiving Day in 1906.

The hospital was modern in every respect, with hot and cold circulating water, bathrooms with flush toilets, and telephone service. Various physicians, individuals, and organizations furnished many of the hospital rooms, while volunteers met day after day for sewing bees, soon filling the shelves of the linen room. The Sisters of St. Benedict managed the hospital, supervised by Sister M. Catherine, the Superior. In 1910 the Sisters of Providence took charge. With their training in hospital work they were able to run the facility on a professional and businesslike basis. A concrete addition was built in 1951 and the original building torn down in 1973. The hospital closed when a new one opened in March 1972. Courtesy of Bunnell Collection, Archives, University of Alaska, Fairbanks

The Garden Island School was a small school in the little community that grew up on the north bank of the Chena. The students have come with a variety of sleds, with dog teams that look suspiciously like family pets, and with Indian-made snowshoes. The teacher in the center of the picture has an admirable full-length fur coat and hat. Courtesy of William Waugaman

This panoramic view of Fairbanks in 1906 was probably taken from the roof of the new St. Joseph's Hospital before the church building was moved across the river in 1911. In four years a substantial community was in place. The bridge across the Chena leads to Turner Street. The photo must have been taken just before the great fire of May 1906, which destroyed much of the business district. It was obviously taken after the ice had gone out and the bridge had been rebuilt but before the area just across the river in the center of the picture had burned. Courtesy of Bunnell Collection, Archives, University of Alaska, Fairbanks

Fires and floods were two perils Fairbanks learned to live with. Both could destroy homes, businesses, and supplies as well as lives, and make life precarious in the isolated community. In May 1906 the main part of the business district from Front Street (First Avenue) to Third was destroyed by a fire that spread rapidly through the dry frame buildings with their sawdust insulation. Rebuilding started the next day.

The classic Fairbanks story is that of Volney Richmond, manager of the N. C. Company, who ordered the bacon in the warehouse used as fuel in the power plant so that water pressure for the fire hoses could be kept up. More of the town would have burned if the bacon hadn't saved the day. *Courtesy of Bunnell Collection, Archives, University of Alaska, Fairbanks*

Women's clothes at the turn of the century were not well suited to the frontier. Here, a narrow path across a slough is negotiated by two well-dressed ladies and a dog who looks a little too disreputable to belong to them. *Courtesy of Bunnell Collection, Archives, University of Alaska, Fairbanks*

St. Mathews Episcopal Church and reading room, and St. Mathews Hospital about 1906. Bishop Peter Trimble Rowe founded the church in 1904. The hospital met an urgent need in the community and served it until 1915. The church also functioned as a reading room for the community (with the chancel screened by a curtain). The reading room was very popular and led to the building of the George C. Thomas Memorial Library, a gift of the secretary of the Episcopal Mission Board. Thomas did not see the library, named after him. The Episcopal Church managed the facility until 1942 when the city of Fairbanks assumed responsibility for operating the library. Courtesy of Bunnell Collection, Archives, University of Alaska, Fairbanks

The Tanana Lumber Company managed by F. G. Noyes, was located on Garden Island. Courtesy of Bunnell Collection, Archives, University of Alaska, Fairbanks

The Fred G. Noyes house on Garden Island was built by the manager of the Tanana Lumber Company, which was also located there. It was an impressive house for its time in Fairbanks and today retains much of its original appearance.

The dining room and parlor were elaborately furnished and the woodwork and paneling in the dining room are particularly impressive. Courtesy of Bunnell Collection, Archives, University of Alaska, Fairbanks

The choir at St. Mathews Episcopal Church, about 1906. The Reverend Charles E. Betticher, the first priest-in-charge, is at the left. Courtesy of Bunnell Collection, Archives, University of Alaska, Fairbanks

The St. Mathews Fair, first held in 1906 by the Ladies of the Guild, was a success that continues annually up to the present. The original three-day fairs were held to support the hospital. Later, as one-day events, they support a variety of activities. This scene is in the Moose Hall. Courtesy of Bunnell Collection, Archives, University of Alaska, Fairbanks

Extreme cold, smoke from wood fires, and the resulting ice fog gave Fairbanks this chilly look at 58 degrees below zero on January 24, circa 1911. The low sun in the south is as high as it will go at this season. Courtesy of William Waugaman

"Halloween Roller Skating Masquerade Carnival 1907, Gordons Roller Rink." For a town that was only four years old, the building and the elaborate party are impressive. There were many activities for families and children as well as the bars usually associated with a new mining camp. Courtesy of Bunnell Collection, Archives, University of Alaska, Fairbanks

A garden party before 1910 brought out the ladies in their summer gowns and elaborate hats. The simple houses were made comfortable and stylish within, and the pleasures and customs of other homes were brought to the new ones in the wilderness. Courtesy of Bunnell Collection, Archives, University of Alaska, Fairbanks

A garden party in early Fairbanks. The house is small and simple, but its well-kept appearance with the neat fence and garden, bordered by a boardwalk, show the best of life in a small town. Courtesy of William Waugaman

Fairbanks Public School
May 20th - 05

"An Alaska Home" about 1910. Great care has been taken to make a comfortable modern home in a small space. The kerosene lamp has a heavy shade and the other cloth shade hanging from the ceiling to the left conceals a lightbulb and its wire. Courtesy of Margaret Lentz Collection, Archives, University of Alaska, Fairbanks

The patriotism and community spirit of the early 1900s showed best on the Fourth of July. Visitors poured in from the creeks on the Tanana Valley Railroad, and parades and races were held on First Avenue in these 1908 scenes. Courtesy of Bunnell Collection, Archives, University of Alaska, Fairbanks

"Fairbanks Public School, May 26th—08." Not much landscaping had yet taken place, but a see-saw had been improvised and two faithful dogs were standing by for the end of the school day.

The Fairbanks Weekly Times in October 1907 described the new school building which was to be occupied by mid-November. It was a seventy-six by sixty-four feet frame structure, two stories high, with basement. The two main floors each had four rooms opening on a central hallway. The building was steamheated and boasted electricity. Besides the boiler room, the basement also contained two separate rooms used as play areas by the children during the cold months. A broad stairway led from the main floor to the upper floor, where the principal's office was located in addition to two high school rooms and a large assembly room. A series of stairways finally led to the cupola towering above the center of the building, where, on clear days, spectators enjoyed a beautiful view of the Tanana Valley.

The course of study provided for four years in the primary and four years in the grammar departments. The high school, although small, offered four years work. It included Latin for the entire course of study or science as an alternative, together with two years of German. Both courses included four years of English, three of mathematics and two of history. The school board required students to complete sixteen credits for graduation, allowing one-half credit for each semester for each course.

The building was used until December 4, 1932, when it was destroyed by fire. Courtesy of Bunnell Collection, Archives, University of Alaska, Fairbanks

Birdseye View of Fairbanks Alaska July 3

A community isolated in the wilderness is shown in this 1908 view taken from the signal tower located across the river from the present Island Homes area. A lumber mill is in the foreground while far to the left can be seen two light parallel lines which are the woodpiles for the N. C. Company power plant. Courtesy of Bunnell Collection, Archives, University of Alaska, Fairbanks

Baseball is a continuing pleasure for many Fairbanksans, whether they play or watch. The midnight ball game on June 21 continues as a Fairbanks tradition, still played during the long hours of daylight during the summers. This game was held in 1909. Courtesy of Clara Rust Collection, Archives, University of Alaska, Fairbanks

The Fairbanks Fire Department in 1907 lined up for this photo. From left to right they are: H. C. Johnson, Jack Diston, Captain Jack Buckley (chief), Fred Douse, Jack Roberts, and Gene Huckens. Courtesy of Ralph MacKay Collection, Archives, University of Alaska, Fairbanks

The City Hall Building which included the Fire Station was on Third Avenue opposite Turner Street. This view looks east toward Cushman Street about 1910. Courtesy of Harrie Hughes Collection, Archives, University of Alaska, Fairbanks

Fairbanks residents line the riverbank April 30, 1907, to watch the spring break-up. Part of the superstructure of the wooden bridge is at the left. The ice often destroyed the pilings, which had to be replaced.

Samson's is in its familiar place; to its right is the Daily Miner-Daily News office. Captain Barnette owned the News and W. F. Thompson the Miner, which was a weekly at the time. The two papers carried on an editorial feud with the

Fairbanks Daily Times. In the center on the far bank is the new St. Joseph's Hospital. The church had not yet been moved across the river. Courtesy of Bunnell Collection, Archives, University of Alaska, Fairbanks

An ice jam across the Chena in early May 1911 caused a major flood. The Claypool Berry house, a tall square building (left) at 1309 First Avenue, had just been built. It was the home of Judge Claypool for many years. The flood was more severe than the usual high-water flooding that Fairbanks was used to, but the town soon recovered. Flooding in later years was relieved by the construction of the Moose Creek Dike and, after the 1967 flood, the Chena Lakes Flood Control Project. Courtesy of Driscoll Collection, Archives, University of Alaska, Fairbanks

Graehl grew up as a small community on the north side of the Chena. A small ferry on an overhead cable made the trip easier for commuters about 1908. Courtesy of Bunnell Collection, Archives, University of Alaska, Fairbanks

Wood was in constant demand in early Fairbanks, and many people made their living by providing the fuel needed for homes, mines, and businesses. The hills around the town were heavily harvested to meet the need. Here L. T. Erwin's teams are drawing 30 cords of wood to the N. C. Company power plant about 1910. The sizes of the loads are 7½, 7, 6, 6, and 3½ cords—probably about a one-day supply. Courtesy of Bunnell Collection, Archives, University of Alaska, Fairbanks

The Richert Farm (left) was near the crossing of Cushman Street and the present Airport Road. He built a greenhouse in 1907 and in 1909 had fifty acres under cultivation. Richert raised tomatoes in the greenhouses and cabbage, potatoes, celery, carrots, and other vegetables which he sold in the town from the back of his wagon.

The Detention Hospital (right) was apparently for the mentally ill and located at what were then the outskirts of town. Courtesy of Norma Hoyt Collection

Ed Bartlett's oatfield near Golden, Alaska, about fifteen miles north of Fairbanks and near the Goldstream mining area about 1906, was a good location to supply the miners and their horses. Today Golden is gone and forest covers the area. Bartlett was the father of E. L. "Bob" Bartlett, Alaska's last delegate to Congress, 1944 to 1958, and the new state's first senior U. S. Senator from 1959 until his death on December 11, 1968. Courtesy of Bunnell Collection, Archives, University of Alaska, Fairbanks

Farming was important in the Fairbanks area as the community tried to supply many of its own food needs. The federal government built an Experimental Farm west of town in 1907. Here a self-binder works a field of oats in 1913. Courtesy of Driscoll Collection, Archives, University of Alaska, Fairbanks

Garden Island was known for its gardens, farms, and greenhouses which supplied much of Fairbanks's vegetables. This farm is probably located behind Samson Hardware in the general area that serves as a community garden today. Courtesy of Bunnell Collection, Archives, University of Alaska, Fairbanks

A farmer with a load of hay behind his mule team. Many horses were used in town until the automobile finally became a practical alternative in the mid-teens. The building has large shutters at its windows to help conserve heat in the cold, dark winter months. Most buildings, even of this size, were insulated with sawdust—which worked quite well but created a fire hazard. Courtesy of Bunnell Collection, Archives, University of Alaska, Fairbanks

William Young's ranch with his team cutting what appear to be oats, probably about 1906. Courtesy of Bunnell Collection, Archives, University of Alaska, Fairbanks

A break-up scene on Fourth Avenue about 1910. The fence across Fourth Avenue at Cushman marked "the line," a section of town reserved for prostitutes. Cribb's building later became Gordon's store. Courtesy of W. F. Erskine Collection, Archives, University of Alaska, Fairbanks

The Tanana Valley Railroad terminal was on Garden Island near the site of the present Fairbanks Daily News-Miner building. It served the many communities of the mining district north of town. Here, an excursion train leaves the station. The building was moved after the Alaska Railroad purchased the Tanana Valley Railroad and was converted to a dormitory. Courtesy of Bunnell Collection, Archives, University of Alaska, Fairbanks

Celebrate the Fourth

IN AN

Adler-Rochester

Stein-Bloch

OR

Stadium Suit

The Best to be Had
for the least money

Suits $15
Suits $20
Suits $25
Suits $35

All at Outside Cost, Freight Added

Trunks, Suit Cases and Grips

M. A. PINSKA;

Fairbanks and Dawson

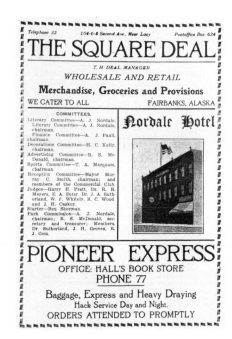

Telephone 32   104-6-8 Second Ave., Near Lacy   Postoffice Box 634

THE SQUARE DEAL

T. H. DEAL, MANAGER

WHOLESALE AND RETAIL

Merchandise, Groceries and Provisions

WE CATER TO ALL   FAIRBANKS, ALASKA

COMMITTEES.

Literary Committee—A. J. Nordale. Literary Committee—A. J. Nordale, chairman.
Finance Committee—A. J. Paull, chairman.
Decorations Committee—H. C. Kelly, chairman.
Advertising Committee—R. S. McDonald, chairman.
Sports Committee—T. A. Marquam, chairman.
Reception Committee—Mayor Murray C. Smith, chairman; and members of the Commercial Club.
Judge—Harry E. Pratt, Dr. R. R. Meyers, E. A. Suter, Dr. J. A. Sutherland, W. F. Whitely, R. C. Wood and J. H. Caskey.
Starter—Ben Sherman.
Park Commission—A. J. Nordale, chairman; R. S. McDonald, secretary and treasurer; Members, Dr. Sutherland, J. H. Groves, R. J. Geis.

Nordale Hotel

PIONEER EXPRESS

OFFICE: HALL'S BOOK STORE

PHONE 77

Baggage, Express and Heavy Draying
Hack Service Day and Night.

ORDERS ATTENDED TO PROMPTLY

Tanana Valley R. R. Co.

Special Train Service for the 4th of July Celebration, 1913

GOING TO FAIRBANKS

Leaves—	CHATANIKA	GILMORE	FOX	ESTER SIDING
JULY 2	7:00 am	8:35 am. 4:05 pm.	8:50 am. 4:20 pm.	9:40 am. 4:55 pm.
JULY 3	7:00 am	7:30 am. 8:35 am. 4:05 pm.	7:45 am. 8:50 am. 4:20 p. m.	8:30 am. 9:40 am. 4:55 pm.
JULY 4	7:00 am	7:30 am. 8:35 am. 11:00 am.	7:45 am. 8:50 am. 11:15 am.	8:30 am. 9:40 am. 12:05 pm.
JULY 5	7:00 am	8:35 am. 4:05 pm.	8:50 am. 4:20 pm.	9:40 am. 4:55 pm.
JULY 6	7:00 am	8:35 am. 4:05 pm.	8:50 am. 4:20 pm.	9:40 am. 4:55 pm.

RETURNING, LEAVE FAIRBANKS.

For—	ESTER SIDING	FOX	GILMORE	CHATANIKA
JULY 2	9:20 am. 4:30 pm.	9:20 am. 4:30 pm.	9:20 am. 4:30 pm.	4:30 pm.
JULY 3	9:20 am. 4:30 pm.	9:20 am. 4:30 pm.	9:20 am. 4:30 pm.	4:30 pm.
JULY 4	9:20 am. 11:00 pm.	9:20 am. 11:00 pm.	9:20 am. 11:00 pm.	11:00 pm.
JULY 5	9:20 am. 4:30 pm. 6:00 pm.	9:20 am. 4:30 pm. 6:00 pm.	9:20 am. 4:30 pm. 6:00 pm.	4:30 pm.
JULY 6	9:20 am. 4:30 pm.	9:20 am. 4:30 pm.	9:20 am. 4:30 pm.	4:30 pm.

NO FREIGHT OF ANY KIND WILL BE HANDLED ON THE 4th AND 5th.

EXCURSION RATES

FROM CHATANIKA TO FAIRBANKS AND RETURN............$4.00
OLNES TO FAIRBANKS AND RETURN $3.50
RIDGETOP TO FAIRBANKS AND RETURN $3.00
GILMORE TO FAIRBANKS AND RETURN..................$2.50
FOX TO FAIRBANKS AND RETURN $1.75

TICKETS ON SALE JULY 2ND, 3RD AND 4TH.

GOOD TO RETURN TO JULY 6TH INCLUSIVE

C. W. JOYNT, Gen. Mgr.

*Ads from the 1913 Fourth of July program.
Courtesy of Archives, University of Alaska,
Fairbanks*

*Tanana Valley Railroad special schedule, 1913.
Courtesy of Archives, University of Alaska,
Fairbanks*

*Auto races were popular on the track in the
cleared area at the end of Cowles Street. This is
probably the July Fourth race in 1915. Tom
Gibson is in car number 3 and Mae Gibson is at
the right. Courtesy of Gibson Collection,
Archives, University of Alaska, Fairbanks*

Women in long dresses and men in suits and hats tried the ice on the river rink below the N. C. Company dock. A photographer is setting up his camera in the foreground and spectators line the temporary bridge. The steamer *Lotta Talbot* is drawn up to the bank for the winter. The photo was probably taken before 1906 since St. Joseph's Hospital is not yet in place on the north bank. *Courtesy of Bunnell Collection, Archives, University of Alaska, Fairbanks*

Tom Gibson with one of his auto stages loaded for a trip along the Richardson. Part of the windshield is raised, perhaps for increased ventilation! Mae Gibson is in the passenger's seat. *Courtesy of Gibson Collection, Archives, University of Alaska, Fairbanks*

The Gibson house on First Avenue with the Gibson Garage and one of the cars used for the transportation company just beyond. The logs look freshly caulked to keep out the cold and drafts, and the rain barrel is in place to save water from the board roof. Mae Gibson is on the porch. *Courtesy of Gibson Collection, Archives, University of Alaska, Fairbanks*

The trails in the Interior needed extensive work before they could qualify as roads. This situation obviously needs a lot of thought before too much effort is put into it. *Courtesy of Archives, University of Alaska, Fairbanks*

Four early curlers with their trophy. Four players make up a "rink" and compete against another rink. The stones and brooms are the curler's basic equipment. *Courtesy of Bunnell Collection, Archives, University of Alaska, Fairbanks*

The rink on the river about 1906 was used by the Fairbanks Curling Club, founded in 1905. Curling, a uniquely northern sport, has continued to the present with international competitions held regularly. In 1981 the club hosted the U. S. Men's National Championships. *Courtesy of Bunnell Collection, Archives, University of Alaska, Fairbanks*

Gibson's Auto Stage caravan left Fairbanks September 10, 1915, for Chitina. There were no bridges, nor many roads at the time. Tom Gibson is shown at the wheel of the first Dodge in Fairbanks. Courtesy of Gibson Collection, Archives, University of Alaska, Fairbanks

Chapter II

GROWING AND CHANGING

1914-1940

Economic conditions continued to deteriorate slowly. When World War I broke out in 1914, high wages and better opportunities lured many Alaskans outside. These were lean years, when the territory's economic and population growth, never spectacular except during the gold stampedes, came to a standstill. Census statistics between 1910 and 1920 showed a drop of 9,320 in the territory's population, and Fairbanks had shrunk to 3,400 in 1910; by 1920 it had dwindled to little more than 1,100 souls. Charley Geis, a town resident during this period, recalled that it was "a very tough time in Fairbanks—people just about existing and that is all." The Alaska Road Commission hired a few men in the summertime and construction of the Alaska Railroad, finally comppleted in 1925, helped a little, but economically the times were tough.

Edby Davis, a high school senior in 1917, remembered that although not much was said in school, "we could see the war clouds coming and with the signing of the draft bill, we boys knew our future was uncertain." On May 15 of that year, the principal called the four graduating seniors into his office and instructed them to plan the commencement program. The Reverend Hope Lumpkin of St. Matthew's Episcopal Church gave the invocation, and then Alta Porter, Rodney Johnson, Earl Focter, and Edby Davis received their diplomas made of moosehide, a custom which ended with the class of 1918.

In the fall Davis registered for the draft, and in the spring of 1918 he observed the first contingent of thirty-eight draftees leave Fairbanks. The steamer *General Jacobs* picked up draftees on its way downriver from Nenana and Tolovana, bound for Fort Gibbon on the Tanana River. At the same time men from Flat, Ophir, and Holy Cross arrived at Fort Gibbon. From there they all went Outside for training. In

Bob Sheldon at the wheel of a car ready for the road. Mrs. Wanamaker is beside him. The two passengers bundled in fur coats in the back and with a fur rug behind them are unidentified. Skis are strapped on the front wheels and chains are on the back tires. Shovel, rope, and a spotlight are all handy on this early spring day. Sheldon's interest in automobiles had led him to build Alaska's first auto in Skagway in 1905 (now in the University Museum). He continued his interest with a stageline on the Richardson Highway to Valdez and later in Mt. McKinley National Park. Courtesy of Mathilde Link-Francine Mears Collection

October of that year, Davis, together with about forty other men, was drafted and eventually reached Fort Lewis, Washington, for training. But before his training was completed, the war ended and Davis returned to Fairbanks in 1919.

In the meantime, Alaska's delegate to Congress, James Wickersham, had successfully put a measure through Congress in 1915 which set aside certain lands in the Tanana Valley for a land-grant college. This enabled the territorial legislature of 1917 to pass a bill establishing the Alaska Agricultural College and School of Mines. Construction of a few buildings some four miles west of Fairbanks on a hill overlooking the town and the Alaska Range began in 1918, but lack of appropriation did not allow completion until 1921. The board of trustees hired Charles E. Bunnell, teacher, businessman, lawyer, and judge to be the institution's chief executive officer. Bunnell took office in December 1921. On September 18, 1922, the college opened its doors for business with a student body of six and six faculty. This one-to-one ratio changed when another six students signed up. The editor of the *Fairbanks Daily News-Miner* observed that the names of these first college students would "live in college history of the Northland when they are gone and their number will be augmented from day to day until that college will have more students than the population of Fairbanks amounts to in the aggregate today." In 1922 the town had a population of about 1,200. University on-campus enrollment did not reach that figure until about 1962.

Another development was the construction of the Alaska Railroad, begun in 1915 by the federal government. President Warren G. Harding drove the golden spike signifying completion at North Nenana on July 15, 1923. The tracks reached Fairbanks in 1925, connecting the town with Anchorage and Seward at tidewater. With the railroad in Fairbanks and the modest growth of the Alaska Agricul-

tural College and School of Mines, the town took a new lease on life. A major development began in Alaska in 1923 when the United States Smelting Refining and Mining Company, a Maine corporation headquartered in Boston, Massachusetts, acquired an interest, and later total ownership, in Hammond Consolidated Gold Fields, operating dredges at Nome. The Fairbanks Exploration Company, a subsidiary of USSR&M, started an extensive prospecting and drilling program in the Fairbanks area in 1924. It subsequently acquired large land holdings on many creeks through option, lease, and purchase. After it had bought out most small operators, the Fairbanks Exploration Company employed large-scale mining methods to extract gold. By 1925 it had become the largest contributor to the economy of interior Alaska, a position it held for many years, until the outbreak of World War II.

The Fairbanks population again grew slowly. In 1926 the town had a population of 1,725, while the company employed a total of 1,372 men in the interior with an annual payroll of $1,032,408. By 1935 the town's population had grown to 2,778 and the company had 903 men, earning $1,955,070 in that year. By 1943 the population in Fairbanks had grown to 4,151, stimulated by the war boom. In that year the company employed a mere 66 men with a payroll of $123,170—the decrease due to Public Law 208, which shut down gold mining for the duration of the war as a nonessential activity. Mining never recovered after the war.

While a revived gold mining industry contributed to the economy of interior Alaska, a revolution in transportation occurred. The airplane connected the territory's isolated settlements and shrank vast distances. Flying actually was not new to Alaskans, however. In the summer of 1913 Captain J. J. Martin and his wife shipped a small plane from the States by way of Skagway over the Yukon and White Pass

58

A new steel bridge replaced the transient wooden structures that spanned the Chena in 1917. Here viewers of the dedication ceremony lined up to try out the new structure and crowded the old wooden bridge leading to Samson's on Garden Island. Courtesy of Driscoll Collection, Archives, University of Alaska, Fairbanks

Railroad and thence down the Yukon and up the Tanana and Chena rivers to Fairbanks. In an aerial circus they demonstrated to the citizens of Alaska's interior what the future might hold.

For Alaskans, "The Aviation," as they called it, was a natural. A vast wilderness separated the small settlements and movement between these settlements was slow. In the summers stern-wheeled steamers, launches, and poling boats floated along the many rivers, but after the fall freeze-up each settlement dug in for a long, cold, and dark winter alone. Dog teams and their drivers struggled along the trails with mail and freight. There was only one railroad of any length in this vast territory, reaching 470 miles from the port of Seward to the interior town of Fairbanks. In the winter, snow slides often closed the route. And in all of Alaska there was only one long road, the Richardson Highway. It was narrow and crooked, and also reached inland to Fairbanks from the Port of Valdez on Prince William Sound. In the summer, cars, with luck, navigated the 360 miles in three days. In the winter, deep snow drifts blocked the road. So it was not long before everybody in Alaska traveled by air, including fishermen and miners, trappers, congressmen, engineers, prostitutes, and salesmen; Indians, Aleuts, Eskimos, and whites all crowded together aloft in the narrow cabins of the airplanes.

Carl Ben Eielson, destined to become America's foremost arctic pilot, arrived in Fairbanks at age twenty-five in 1922 to teach science and mathematics in the high school. In 1917 he had enlisted in the U. S. Army, joining the aerial force, and soon became an instructor in aeronautics. Eielson left the service with the rank of lieutenant. While teaching high school, Eielson persuaded a group of the town's businessmen, foremost among them the pioneer banker Dick Wood, to put up the money for a plane. He ordered a Jenny with an OX-5 engine, which

arrived crated at the Fairbanks depot on July 1, 1923. Eielson assembled it and three days later climbed into the wicker seat of the open cockpit plane for the first commercial flight in interior Alaska. That summer he made several cross-country trips hauling passengers and light freight to nearby towns.

In the fall of 1923, after much effort, Eielson persuaded the United States Post Office Department to award him an air mail contract for ten twice-monthly mail trips from Fairbanks to McGrath, some 300 miles distant. The contractor also agreed to ship him a Liberty-powered DeHavilland and pay him two dollars a mile—less than half the cost of mail delivered by sled dog. On February 21, 1924, Eielson made his first mail delivery to McGrath, followed by others, until he cracked up his plane in Fairbanks. The Post Office Department refused to supply parts or to finance the repairs. With two more flights in his contract to go, Eielson had to ship the DeHavilland back to the States.

Eielson then left for Washington, D.C., to lobby for government air service in Alaska, but was unsuccessful. He did not return to Alaska until 1926, and then as a pilot for the expedition Captain George Wilkins had organized to fly over the Arctic Ocean. Eventually, there were three expeditions, and Wilkins and Eielson, the former as navigator and the latter as pilot, logged a total of 500 hours aloft, making history in the process.

In 1928 Eielson and Wilkins finally crossed the top of the world in a Lockheed Vega monoplane, powered with a Wright J-5 engine. Other exploits followed, but in 1929 Eielson returned to Fairbanks as the vice president and general manager of Alaskan Airways, a subsidiary of the New York-based Aviation Corporation which had bought and merged several Alaskan pioneer firms. On his first contract, taking off passengers and furs from the American trading motorship *Nanuk,* ice-bound off the village of

Mrs. Thomas Markham hosted a group of pioneers at the Markham home in 1914. The party consisted of men who had come to the Yukon before 1890. The year they came to the Yukon and the year they died follows their names, from left to right: Andrew Jackson Maiden, 1886-1915; Hans Madsen, 1876-1931; Captain Al Mayo, 1873-1922; William H. McPhee, 1888-1934; Jim Bender, 1886-1932. Courtesy of Archives, University of Alaska Fairbanks

The Ladies Aid of the Presbyterian Church in 1914. Mrs. D. Driscoll, second from the left in the second row, was the president. Courtesy of Driscoll Collection, Archives, University of Alaska, Fairbanks

North Cape, Siberia, Eielson and his mechanic, Earl Borland, crashed and died. After an extensive international search, Alaskan pilots Joe Crosson and Harold Gillam found Eielson's wreck on January 25, 1930. The bodies were not uncovered until about a month later.

In the meantime, Jimmy Rodebaugh organized the Alaska Aerial Transportation Company in early 1924 and hired a couple of young farm boys, Noel Wien and Arthur Sampson, to fly the two Standards. Early in 1925 citizens of the town decided to establish the Fairbanks Airplane Company, in which Rodebaugh became the biggest stockholder. The new company abandoned the ball park (1,400 feet long with stumps and a high woodpile at one end) which had served as an airfield and smoothed out a real field from a vacant lot at the edge of town. And although there were many crashes, and many small companies formed, went broke, and reorganized again, "The Aviation" had arrived in Alaska to stay.

As early as 1931 the governor of Alaska reported to the secretary of the interior that the territory occupied a strategic position on the only feasible air route to Asia. Despite the fact that increasing numbers of aircraft passed through Alaska each year along this route and improved facilities were desirable, the federal government had taken little interest in promoting aviation in the territory. The governor urged the Army Air Corps to station planes in the north, if for no other reason

The stands were full for this game on July 4, 1919. The new ball park was at the end of Cowles and Barnette streets in the Weeks Field area. Courtesy of Clara Rust Collection, Archives, University of Alaska, Fairbanks

This photograph is simply labeled "George and Martha, Feb. 22, 1915." The elaborate costumes must have been for a special celebration of Washington's birthday. Courtesy of Driscoll Collection, Archives, University of Alaska, Fairbanks

than to train their pilots in arctic and subarctic flying conditions, but the recommendations fell on deaf ears. Anthony J. Dimond, Alaska's delegate to congress, in 1934 warned of the danger of Japanese invasion and asked that military bases be established at Anchorage and Fairbanks, and also in the Aleutians. Dimond pointed out that the shortest distance between the United States and the Orient lay over the Great Circle Route. From San Francisco to Yokohama the shortest route was 5,223 miles; from Seattle only 4,924 miles. Dimond asked for an appropriation of $10 million for an Alaska air base. His bills for an air and a naval base were referred to the House Military and Naval Affairs committees, respectively, and died there.

In 1935, however, Congress provided for the expansion of air defenses in the United States. It named six strategic areas in each of which there would be an Army Air Corps base and also planned for intermediate stations. Alaska was to be one of these areas.

The military brass supported an Alaskan base, and pointed out that it was sorely needed for defensive-offensive purposes and to provide training in cold-weather aviation. Most important, however, was the testimony of Brigadier General William Mitchell on February 13, 1935. He testified at length and forcefully on the importance and value of air power in war. Mitchell predicted the strategic importance of Alaska in the coming era of air power, whose prophet he was. He declared that Japan was America's most dangerous enemy in the Pacific. "They won't attack Panama. They will come right here to Alaska. Alaska is the most central place in the world for aircraft, and that is true either of Europe, Asia, or North America. I believe in the future he who holds Alaska will hold the world, and I think it is the most important strategic place in the world."

But despite favorable testimony and earnest pleading from Delegate Dimond, Congress did not act. It was not until 1940 that Congress appropriated $4 million and construction began near Fairbanks, not of a base but rather a cold-weather testing station, to be named Ladd Field.

It took 8,000 to 9,000 cords of wood each year to furnish the power for Fairbanks in the early 1920s. The N. C. Company maintained a wood yard on the south side of town where a supply was built up and brought to the plant in town on cars pulled along the tracks visible between the rows of logs in this view about 1918. The school building is at the right and the steel bridge is visible in the distance.

By the second decade of the twentieth century, Fairbanks experienced an acute fuel shortage as most of the accessible timber had been cut. The Alaska Railroad, which reached Fairbanks in 1925, connected the town to the Healy lignite coal fields and ended the fuel shortage. Courtesy of Archives, University of Alaska, Fairbanks

Roden Davis worked at the N. C. power plant, where impressive furnaces were beginning to use coal from the Healy fields in the mid-1920s. The use of coal was made possible by the completion of the Alaska Railroad. Courtesy of Evolyn Melville Collection

"First quota National Army Local Board No. 17, Fairbanks, Alaska, inducted June 27th, 1918." World War I had a major effect on the town, with many men leaving and gold mining slowing down. Two brighter events were the construction of the Alaska Railroad and the founding of the Agricultural College and School of Mines during this period. Courtesy of William Waugaman

Edby David graduated from Fairbanks High School in 1917. The diplomas that year were made of moosehide with decorated covers. Margaret Keenan was the principal; Cora N. Hamilton, the president of the Board of Education; and A. R. Heilig clerk. Courtesy of University of Alaska Museum

The Pioneer Brewing Company, which followed the Arctic Brewing Company and the Barthel Brewing Company produced Midnight Sun Beer, popular throughout the Interior. The Barthel Brewing Company put bottled beer on the market October 13, 1906, and rated a news item in the **Fairbanks Weekly Times**: "The Barthel Brewing Company will begin the sale of case lots to families this afternoon." The company's slogan was "Everyone can have a bottle." In 1936 the Fairbanks brewery burned to the ground, causing estimated damage of $70,000. It was never rebuilt. Courtesy of University of Alaska Museum

A winter scene at Berry, later Ester, a mining camp about twelve miles west of Fairbanks. The camp was first named for the Berry brothers. Clarence J. Berry developed the thaw point and after doing well in Dawson and Fairbanks continued his success in California. The C. J. Berry Holding Company provided support for the popular gold exhibit at the University Museum. Courtesy of Herbert Heller Collection, Archives, University of Alaska, Fairbanks

This view of Cushman Street from Second Avenue about 1915 shows the unpaved streets with their wooden crosswalks and a city water main valve in the foreground. Courtesy of Archives, University of Alaska, Fairbanks

This photograph from the 1920s may have been taken in the gymnasium of the old Main High School at a Thanksgiving celebration (note the turkeys on the tablecloth). Most of those identified are in the group in the left foreground. Mrs. Mary Miller is seated in the center of that group wearing a light-colored scarf. To the right of Mrs. Miller, with his elbow on the table, is Mr. Ballaine, who had a farm on Farmer's Loop Road. The small lake along that road and a road leading to the Goldstream Valley bear his name. The man behind him is Bobby Sheldon. The woman with the two white stripes on the bodice of her dress is Florence Ross Thompson, one of the early graduates of the Alaska Agricultural College and School of Mines. At the extreme right with her head turned away is Albina Miller, one of Mrs. Miller's daughters. Miller Hill Road, just west of the university, was named for the Miller's, whose homestead it borders. Courtesy of Norma Hoyt Collection

Tanana Valley Lodge No. 162 Free and Accepted Masons presided at the laying of the Cornerstone of the Alaska Agricultural College and School of Mines on July 4, 1915. John W. Buckley, in top hat, was acting worshipful master and is shown preparing the box of documents to be placed in the cornerstone. Dedication of the college and the start of classes did not take place until September, 1922. The first and only graduate in 1923 was John Sexton Shanly. Courtesy of Historic Photograph Collection, Archives, University of Alaska, Fairbanks

Dedication Day, September 13, 1922. Gathering to wait for the governor's motorcade. Courtesy of Bunnell Collection, Archives, University of Alaska, Fairbanks

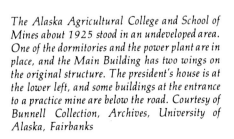

College Road, leading up the hill to the campus, is no longer a public access road. The college used the buildings at the entrance to the mine tunnel, a teaching mine for students. Courtesy of Heller Collection, Archives, University of Alaska, Fairbanks

The Alaska Agricultural College and School of Mines about 1925 stood in an undeveloped area. One of the dormitories and the power plant are in place, and the Main Building has two wings on the original structure. The president's house is at the lower left, and some buildings at the entrance to a practice mine are below the road. Courtesy of Bunnell Collection, Archives, University of Alaska, Fairbanks

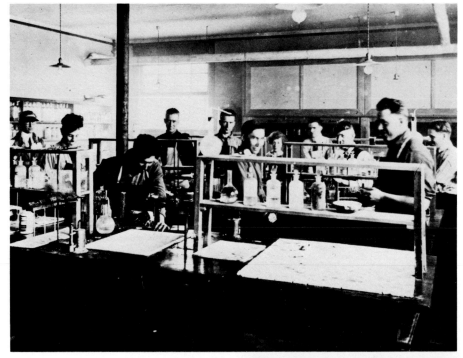

A chemistry class in the 1920s. This story is told about Dr. Bunnell: When visitors came to campus, students would rush to the lab to tinker with vials and bunsen burners. Dr. Bunnell would guide the visitors past the bustling classroom with its scientific equipment, and the visitors would leave favorably impressed with the work being done on campus. Courtesy of Archives, University of Alaska, Fairbanks

The first college basketball team 1922-23. From left to right, standing: Professor Earl Pilgrim, Bob McCombe, Art Loftus, Ted Loftus, and Jules Loftus, John McCombe. Kneeling: Roden Davis and Jack Hosler. Earl Pilgrim, in his late eighties, still mines in the wilderness north of Fairbanks at his Stampede mine. Courtesy of William Waugaman

Male students and faculty on the steps of the old Main in the 1930s. Courtesy of Frank Pettygrove Collection, Archives, University of Alaska, Fairbanks

Carolyn Chase about 1928 on the running board of Dr. Bunnell's 1926 Buick. Courtesy of Dr. Roland Chase Collection, Archives, University of Alaska, Fairbanks

Lydia Jacobson (Fohn-Hansen) about 1927-28 in warm winter parka, hat, and mitts. Mrs. Fohn-Hansen was with the U. S. Extension Service and taught home economics at the university for many years. Now retired, as Associate Director of Cooperative Extension, Emeritus, she continues to be active in national organizations for retired people. Courtesy of Dr. Roland Chase Collection, Archives, University of Alaska, Fairbanks

Dorothy Roth and Arthur W. Loftus, students at the college, on a 1925 field trip in the Alaska Range. Dorothy graduated from the college in 1927. Art was the fifth student to enroll at the college when he first attended in 1922. They were married in 1928. Courtesy of William Cashen Collection, Archives, University of Alaska, Fairbanks

In front of the Fairbanks depot is the "Brill" Car which served as a commuter train for college faculty and students who lived in town. Engine No. 1 of the Tanana Valley Railroad was set up as a memorial just in front of the Cushman Street Bridge. Art Marsh was one of the early drivers of the car. Courtesy of Historical Photograph Collection, Archives, University of Alaska, Fairbanks

The lobby of one of the hotels or one of the lodges. Electric lights, comfortable chairs, and an assortment of reading material on the table and in the wall rack made this a welcome change from the small cabins of the creeks. Courtesy of Bunnell Collection, Archives, University of Alaska, Fairbanks

The Curling Club had constructed an indoor rink on Second Avenue between Cowles and Wickersham in 1908. This is an early view of that building with its two sheets of natural ice. Courtesy of Bunnell Collection, Archives, University of Alaska, Fairbanks

A flood in the early 1920s inundated Samson's on Garden Island but not the slightly higher south bank of the river. Floods were a continuing worry to the low-lying town. Courtesy of Herbert Heller Collection, Archives, University of Alaska, Fairbanks

The Richardson Highway, leading to Valdez, was a major route developing from a trail used by stampeders to the Fairbanks camp. Auto stages and freight lines replaced horse-drawn wagons and sleighs. Until the earthquake of 1964, which totally destroyed the town, Valdez was a major supply port for Fairbanks and the Interior. Courtesy of Driscoll Collection, Archives, University of Alaska, Fairbanks

A Richardson Highway construction crew and their equipment outside the Third Avenue Bath House in the 1920s. The bath house was on Cushman between Third and Fourth avenues. Courtesy of Norma Hoyt Collection

The Fairbanks depot was built in 1923 and used until the late 1950s. The whole area has since been changed with the **Fairbanks Daily News-Miner** building in about this spot and the new Alaska Railroad station to the north of it. Courtesy of Reuel Griffin Collection, Archives, University of Alaska, Fairbanks

The Richardson Highway Transportation Company shared this neat building on the northwest corner of Second and Lacy streets in the late 1920s with the Fairbanks Tourist Bureau.

Two of their comfortable "stages" full of passengers are waiting on the yet-unpaved street. The Polaris Building now occupies the site. Courtesy of Helen L. Atkinson Collection

The Gibson Stage Line traveled the Richardson Highway to Valdez in the 1920s. The road was a big improvement over the trail the stampeders had used twenty years before but still was a rough trip for vehicles and passengers. Roy Hoyt, the driver, stands on the running board while passengers explore the roadside. Courtesy of Norma Hoyt Collection

A view of Garden Island after the 1923 Fairbanks Depot was constructed by the Alaska Railroad. Several of the buildings in the row had been moved across the tracks from a previous location in the area on this side of the depot. Courtesy of Driscoll Collection, Archives, University of Alaska, Fairbanks

The Dr. J. R. Sutherland residence was at the corner of First and Cowles. Nora I. Sutherland was noted for her fancy needlework, which is evident in this view of their parlor and dining room in the 1920s. The house was torn down in 1976. Courtesy of Tanana Valley Fair Association

A spring goose hunt in the early 1920s (near 10 mile on the old Richardson Highway.) It looks like Tom Gibson's old Dodge behind, left to right: Forbes Baker, Lou Joy, Jess Rust, and Adolph Murie. Game was a welcome supplement to menus, particularly after a long winter with limited fresh food. Courtesy of Evolyn Melville Collection

"Thawing a Fairbanks sewer." The steam boiler mounted on a sled was used to thaw frozen pipes. For many years most Fairbanks residences relied upon their own septic systems. This picture was probably taken in the mid-1920s. Courtesy of Reuel Griffin Collection, Archives, University of Alaska, Fairbanks

A 1924 aerial view shows the steel bridge with the N. C. Company buildings on the right. The bridge leads to Cushman Street. The next short street to the right is Turner Street and the City Hall can be seen at the end of that street on Third Avenue. Courtesy of Norma Hoyt Collection

A parade on June 21, 1924, included this prize-winning float decorated with ribbons and mounted ptarmigan. Courtesy of Norma Hoyt Collection

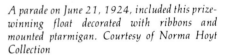

FAIRBANKS ALASKA

A view of Fairbanks in the early 1920s. Cushman and Eighth Avenue cross at the lower right corner of the picture. The Presbyterian Church with its steeple was a landmark on Cushman. The buildings in the foreground show a typical building style with successive additions to the original building. In the winter every house depended on its own wood fire, and a pall of smoke hung over the town in the still air. Courtesy of Herbert Heller Collection, Archives, University of Alaska, Fairbanks

FAIRBANKS, ALASK

The Nordale Hotel fire destroyed the building on First Avenue in about 1924. The Fairview Hotel was about where the USO is now located. Fires were a continual hazard in the wood-structured community with wood-fire heaters in heavy use. Courtesy of Norma Hoyt Collection

The City Hall in the early 1920s held the fire department with its modern equipment. Two of the vehicles carry advertising signs saying "Goodyear Tires, Samson Hardware Co." The building was located on Third Avenue opposite Turner Street. The young boy on the left is in complete uniform, too. Courtesy of Norma Hoyt Collection

At the Tanana Valley Fair held in the Moose Hall in 1924, the needlework exhibit was a prominent feature. The hall later became the Wickersham Apartments, which were torn down in 1976. Courtesy of Tanana Valley Fair Association

President Warren G. Harding came to Fairbanks after driving the symbolic spike to complete the Alaska Railroad at Nenana. He spoke to an attentive crowd at the Fairbanks baseball park in July 1923. Alaskans' hopes that their situation would be understood in Washington were dashed when Harding died on his return trip. Courtesy of Mrs. George L. Keys Collection, Archives, University of Alaska, Fairbanks

William Fentress Thompson (sometimes called Wrong Font) assumed control of the Fairbanks Daily News in 1906, and until his death in 1926 was the major newspaper man in Fairbanks. He kept the newspapers that evolved into The Fairbanks Daily News-Miner. He always had advice and opinions he was willing to share with the community. Fairbanksans fondly remember the controversial newspaper man for his imagination and love for the city. Courtesy of Norma Hoyt Collection

The Empress Theatre, under construction in 1927, was the first building in Fairbanks of reinforced concrete. The steel trusses spanned forty seven feet over the main floor and balcony. The building could seat 670 people. It was used as a theatre until 1961, when it was remodeled for use as the Co-op Drugstore. Courtesy of Bunnell Collection, Archives, University of Alaska, Fairbanks

Bob and Vide Bartlett. Bartlett was a newspaper reporter in Fairbanks before going to Washington to work with Anthony J. Dimond, Alaska's delegate to Congress, in 1933. After mining and several public service jobs, Bartlett returned to Washington as delegate to Congress from 1944 to 1958. He served as U. S. Senator after statehood from 1959 to 1968. A statue of him is in the rotunda of the Capitol in Washington, D.C. Courtesy of Archives, University of Alaska, Fairbanks

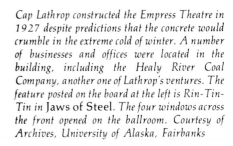

Cap Lathrop constructed the Empress Theatre in 1927 despite predictions that the concrete would crumble in the extreme cold of winter. A number of businesses and offices were located in the building, including the Healy River Coal Company, another one of Lathrop's ventures. The feature posted on the board at the left is Rin-Tin-Tin in Jaws of Steel. The four windows across the front opened on the ballroom. Courtesy of Archives, University of Alaska, Fairbanks

An Eielson flight in 1924. The coming of aviation put the isolated communities of the Interior in closer contact. Mail, supplies, and people began to move more freely and quickly across the roadless areas where transportation had been confined to rivers and trails. The community came out to watch the early flights—and often helped with auto headlights and bonfires to light the field on dark nights, or to help pull the pilot from the plane after some landings. This must have been a special occasion with the men in suits and the women in attractive coats and hats. Courtesy of Norma Hoyt Collection

Carl Ben Eielson stands (in cap) near the cockpit of the Liberty-powered DeHavilland plane that he used on the pioneer mail flights in Alaska in February 1924. Charles Schiek, a Fairbanks carpenter made the large hickory skis. The first flight to McGrath ended with a crash, but the plane was repaired to fly more mail runs and survive more crash landings until a final one that badly damaged it and caused the cancellation of the contract with the Post Office Department. To the right are Frank McCafferty (in cockpit), Mail Inspector Witzler, Harry Watson, Ray Hoyt, and an unidentified man. Dogteams like the one in the background on the right had carried the mails, but now the use of planes made them obsolete. Schiek is standing just in front of the wing. Courtesy of Norma Hoyt Collection

The Bennett-Rodebaugh Company team. Left to right: Matt Niemenan, A. A. Bennett, Carl Ben Eielson, George E. "Ed" Young, and Jimmy Rodebaugh in 1925. The company provided commercial air transportation. Courtesy of F. E. Young Collection, Archives, University of Alaska, Fairbanks

Some of the hangars in the Weeks Field area. The group to the left belongs to Wien Alaska Airlines, while the building to the left is Pollock Air Service. Courtesy of Reuel Griffin Collection, Archives, University of Alaska, Fairbanks

The Alaskan Airways hangar in the Weeks Field area in 1929 with a Stearman and two Fairchild 71s. The hanger has a unique weathervane in the shape of a plane. Courtesy of F. E. Young Collection, Archives, University of Alaska, Fairbanks

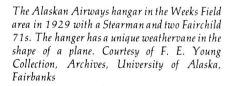

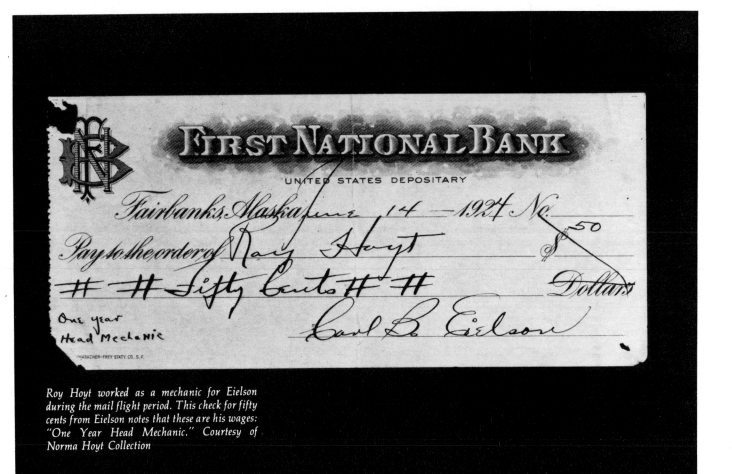

Roy Hoyt worked as a mechanic for Eielson during the mail flight period. This check for fifty cents from Eielson notes that these are his wages: "One Year Head Mechanic." Courtesy of Norma Hoyt Collection

Earl Borland, a young mechanic, accompanied Eielson on his final fatal flight. The picture is inscribed "To Ray from Irene 2-15-30." Borland's body had been located February 13 in the snows off the Siberian coast. Roy Hoyt, a friend of Borland's, received this memento from Borland's widow. Courtesy of Norma Hoyt Collection

Captain Hubert Wilkins and Carl Ben Eielson with the Wright-motored Lockheed Vega used in the first flight over the North Pole in 1928 from Point Barrow to Spitzbergen. Courtesy of F. E. Young Collection, Archives, University of Alaska, Fairbanks

Pilot Noel Wien in 1927 in the first cabin plane with an air-cooled engine in Alaska, a four place Stinson, used by Sir Hubert Wilkins on three flights to Barrow and sold to the Wiens in 1927. It was used for the first scheduled flights to Nome. Courtesy of Noel Wien Collection, Archives, University of Alaska, Fairbanks

This 1929 photo shows Jim Hutchison, S. E. Robbins, Jerry Jones, and Ed Young in front of the Alaskan Airways Stearman plane. Hutchison still works in the machine shop for Alaska International Air in 1981. The Hutchison Career Center in College is named for Hutchison, who has been involved with Alaskan aviation since his arrival in Alaska with the Army Signal Corps in 1919. Courtesy of F. E. Young Collection, Archives, University of Alaska, Fairbanks

This aerial view, probably about 1927, shows Garden Island and the Wickersham Street area in the foreground. The F. E. Company office building in the upper center is complete but the F. E. power plant does not appear finished. The large building in the lower center is the Moose Hall, later the Wickersham Apartments, which is now gone. Courtesy of Herbert Heller Collection, Archives, University of Alaska, Fairbanks

The Fairbanks kindergarten outside Lumpkin Hall at St. Mathews Episcopal Church about 1928. Left to right, front row: Carrie Chase, Mary Lewis, Helen Baker, Bobby Jay, Muriel Marsh, Earl Grandison, Beverly Barrack, Betty Driscoll, Dorothy Mayo, Jackie Driscoll, Florence Preston, and Vance MacDonald. Back row: Forbes Baker, Shirley Fravel, Jimmy Miller, Marion Fravel, Danny Beyers, Barbara Barrack, Nancy Earling, Bonnie Barrack, Agnes Hanson Marjorie Matschman, Alice Haslem, unidentified, and Blanche Burns. Courtesy of Evolyn Melville Collection

Second Avenue, looking east from Cushman, has none of the old businesses left, but the Empress Theatre building is still recognizable. Also to be seen are the Tanana Bakery, Tavern Rest, Meat Market, Empress Theatre, Imperial Cigar Store, Mrs. Robertsons, Gilsher's Tin Shop, Nordale Hotel, and the Fairbanks Laundry. The picture was taken on a Sunday morning when there was little traffic. Courtesy of Driscoll Collection, Archives, University of Alaska, Fairbanks

Sig Wien shows off a snuggly wrapped Merrill L. Wien in the sled in the late 1920s. Courtesy of Helen L. Atkinson Collection

The 1930 Fairbanks High School men's basketball team included, left to right: Austin Gibbs, Pat Thompson, Gene Crossett, Paul Lein, Arnold Anderson, Jimmy Stewart, and Harold Newton. Their coach was Theodore Gentry. Courtesy of Helen L. Atkinson Collection

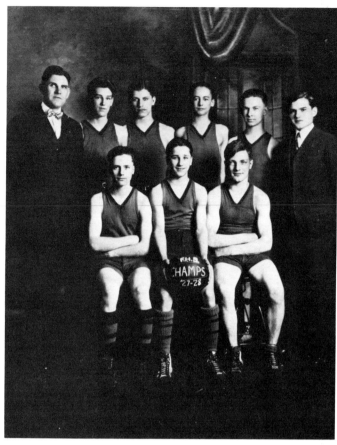

The Fairbanks High School basketball champs, 1927-28. Standing from left to right are Harry Moore, superintendent of schools; Bill Burns; John Butrovich; Austin Gibbs; Paul Solka; and Ted Gentry, coach. Seated are Leonard E. "Pat" Thompson; Henry Miller (who later became an admiral in the U. S. Navy); and Donald M. Hering. Courtesy of Frank Pettygrove Collection, Archives, University of Alaska, Fairbanks

The women's basketball team of Fairbanks High School posed with their coach and advisor in 1930. They are, left to right, back row: Theodore Gentry (coach), Helen Linck, Winifred McDonald, Virginia Riviers (captain), Muriel Riviers, and Marie Bouks (advisor and home economics teacher). In the front row are Sylvia Schmidt, Emma Miller, Becky Hopkins, and Kathryn Scheffler. Courtesy of Helen L. Atkinson Collection

The U. S. Wireless Station "on the Tanana below the Busby ranch." Courtesy of Driscoll Collection, Archives, University of Alaska, Fairbanks

The Nordale Hotel in its new location on Second Avenue. The Gibson Auto Line car is ready for a trip. In the back seat are Alfred E. Brooks, head of the U.S. Geological Survey for Alaska, and Mr. Brownell, secretary to the secretary of the interior. Ray Hoyt is the driver. A distinguished group of Fairbanks businessmen is seeing them off. Brooks was responsible for many of the early geological surveys in the territory, exploring and mapping areas and resources. The Memorial Mines Building at the University, completed in 1952, is named for him. Courtesy of Norma Hoyt Collection

Stampeders were bound for the Salcha River following the news of a goldstrike. Elim Harnish, who served as a model for the character Burning Daylight in Jack London's novel, is in the foreground, about 1926. The hope for a gold strike never dies. Courtesy of Driscoll Collection, Archives, University of Alaska, Fairbanks

The Davidson Ditch was designed to carry water from the Chatanika River to the F. E. grounds near Fairbanks. Here, a siphon crosses the Chatanika River. The ditch was completed in 1928. Courtesy of Archives, University of Alaska, Fairbanks

Joe Hopkins built this "bug" in about 1929. He sits proudly behind the wheel while his sister, Rebecca, sits in the back. Next to Joe is Betty Scheffler Clark, who later became alumni association director for the University of Alaska. Courtesy of Helen L. Atkinson Collection

This aerial view from the late 1920s shows the complex of N. C. Company buildings in the center. Those facing the river have not yet been joined together to form the large building that today serves Nordstrom. The railroad station is at the bottom center, and the little Tanana Valley Railroad engine is just above it in the picture. It remained at that site until 1966, when it was moved to Alaskaland. The docks and warehouses along the riverbank are gone, but a lone sternwheeler is pulled up to the shore at the right, just across the river from the George C. Thomas Memorial Library. Courtesy of Helen L. Atkinson Collection

In the late 1920s large dredges replaced the small gold operations of previous years. The dredge, which floated in a small pond, dug the thawed ground with a bucket line (at the right) and after processing to remove the gold, deposited the tailings behind the dredge. The peculiar pattern is made as the dredge moves forward and a conveyor, swinging from side to side, deposits the tailings behind. This dredge was in the Goldstream area. Courtesy of McAnerney Collection, Archives, University of Alaska, Fairbanks

The Fairbanks Exploration Company office staff in the mid-1930s posed in front of the office building on Illinois Street. Left to right they are, front row: Jack Boswell, Jim Crawford, Agnes Mapelton, Agnes Hering Schlotfeldt, Hertha Baker, and Jack Weaver. Middle row: Burt Ogborn, Charlie Fowler, Arnold Nordale, Cap Osborne, Jim Newlin, and Ross Kirshenbroker. The four men in the back row are: unidentified, Art Daily, Frank Butterfield, and Jack Linck. The others are unidentified. Courtesy of Evolyn Melville Collection

Jim Newlin, who worked for the Fairbanks Exploration Company for many years, poses here with a mammoth skull and tusks about 1930. Workers frequently uncovered Pleistocene fossils during the gold mining operations north of Fairbanks. Interior Alaska was relatively ice-free during the ice ages of the Pleistocene, and many large animals, such as mammoths and super-bison, roamed the area at that time. Their remains are found in the frozen muck that must be cleared to get at the gold-bearing gravel beneath it. Courtesy of Helen L. Atkinson Collection

Harry B. Avakoff, a jeweler and watchmaker in Fairbanks for many years, stood proudly in front of his store at Second and Cushman. Courtesy of Harrie Hughes Collection, Archives, University of Alaska, Fairbanks

Mr. and Mrs. William J. McCurdy brave -42 degree weather to pose for this photo in February 1932. Courtesy of Archives, University of Alaska, Fairbanks

"Uncle Bud" Lauerman and his horse, Nellie, were a familiar sight in Fairbanks. They hauled around a saw mounted on a sled to cut people's wood right at their homes. Mary Ann Link is riding on the saw. The car behind them is decorated for a parade. Courtesy of Mathilde Link-Francine Mears Collection.

Fred Musjerd was the water man for many years, and his business, the "Blue Crystal Wells," provided Fairbanksans with clear water in the 1920s and 1930s. The wagon in this pre-1910 photograph probably predates Musjerd's wells. The note reads: "Dear Cora, this is the way our water wagon looks when its 40 below. We pay 10 cents a pail for water." Most Fairbanks wells produced a brown liquid, heavy with iron and organic matter. In the winter, heaters kept the water from freezing as the water man made his rounds. Courtesy of Bunnell Collection, Archives, University of Alaska, Fairbanks

Mathilde "Tillie" Ertel came to the United States from Germany and met Frank Link in Baltimore, where they married. In 1933 Frank came to Fairbanks at the suggestion of his brother, Paul, who was attending the Alaska Agricultural College and School of Mines. Tillie and Mary Ann followed, and they made their first home in the Kitty Hensley house (now at Alaskaland). With a second daughter, Francine, they lived for many years at the house Frank built in 1938 at 213 Dunkel Street. This photograph shows the newlywed Links in 1930, before they moved to Alaska. Courtesy of Mathilde Link-Francine Mears Collection

The ski slide to the Chena River, shown in March 1934, was located at the present site of the Chamber of Commerce log cabin. The slide was erected as part of the Winter Carnival during its first year. The carnival and many other social events of the 1930s brought the small community together in a close-knit group. The Fairbanks of the 1980s still retains a certain cohesion unusual in towns of this size. Courtesy of Evolyn **Melville Collection**

The ski cabin on Birch Hill was a gathering place for local skiers who skied from town and climbed the slope before making their runs. There were no tows, but judging by the number of skis, it was a popular sport in the mid-1930s. Courtesy of Evolyn Melville Collection

A picnic on the Baker family homestead at the edge of 14 Mile Slough near the present North Pole Junior High School. Left to right: Hertha, Forbes D., Evolyn, Forbes L. and Helen. Many homesteads in the area have become part of developing communities or subdivisions. Courtesy of Evolyn Melville Collection

George A. Parks (standing behind tire) was known as Alaska's flying governor for his travels around the territory. He served as governor from 1925 to 1933. Others in the picture are, left to right: Lynn Smith, U. S. Marshall for the Fourth Judicial Division, Fairbanks 1926-1933; an unidentified Fairbanks High School teacher; Mr. Hawkswork, superintendent, BIA; Governor Parks; unidentified Fairbanks High School teacher; and Ed Young, pilot. Courtesy of F. E. Young Collection, Archives, University of Alaska, Fairbanks

Wiley Post made an historic round-the-world-trip in his plane, the Winnie Mae, in 1933. After a crash at Flat, Alaska, emergency repairs were made with the help of Joe Crosson, a Fairbanks pilot so the flight could continue to Fairbanks and further repairs before going on to New York to complete the record-breaking flight. Courtesy of F. E. Young Collection, Archives, University of Alaska, Fairbanks

Two commemorative envelopes from the first airmail flight between Fairbanks and Juneau were dated May 8, 1938. Robert E. Sheldon was the Fairbanks postmaster from 1933 to 1940. Harry G. Watson, to whom the envelopes are addressed, was secretary to Governor John W. Troy. The second envelope also commemorates the first mail flights in Alaska by Carl Ben Eielson in 1924. Airmail postage was six cents. Courtesy of Norma Hoyt Collection

The Fokker was one of two planes of the Detroit Arctic Expedition which was organized to fly over the Arctic Ocean in 1926. The commander of the expedition was Captain George Hubert Wilkins, an Australian explorer and flyer. After accidents in Fairbanks, the expedition made several flights to Barrow in the Alaskan, a sister ship to the Detroiter. In 1927 their new plane crashed north of Barrow on the pack ice, and Wilkins and Eielson walked for thirteen days to Beechey Point before they were rescued. They planned to return again in 1928. Courtesy of Norma Hoyt Collection

Ed Young, pilot, with Leonard Seppala, the famous dog musher who helped carry serum to Nome during the influenza epidemic in 1925. Seppala is lifting his daughter from the cabin. The plane and hangar belonged to the Bennett-Rodebaugh Company, Inc. Courtesy of F. E. Young Collection, Archives, University of Alaska, Fairbanks

Will Rogers (left) and Wiley Post (second from right) stopped in Fairbanks on their ill-fated trip to Barrow, where they crashed and died. They visited Leonard Seppala, the dog musher (second from left), and Joe Crosson, a Fairbanks pilot (right), on their stop in 1935. Courtesy of Evolyn Melville Collection

Ice hockey on the river in the early 1930s, downstream from the Cushman Street Bridge. The river was wider than today, carried more water, and froze solidly, so it could be used for many winter events. Flood control projects have impacted the river, and the discharge of cooling water and treated sewage has warmed the river. The row of false-fronted buildings in the 700 block of First Avenue included the Hotel Northern, the Pioneer Hotel, and the Hotel Alaska. They are all gone. The Sheet Metal Works in the next block was moved to Alaskaland but burned there shortly after the move. Just beyond it in the center of the picture is the Masonic Temple, which the Masons have used since 1908. The Tanana Commercial Company was originally built in 1906. Courtesy of Helen L. Atkinson Collection

This aerial view was taken before 1932; the old school is still standing in the center right. Cowles Street leads to the open area where hangars share space with a set of bleachers at the ball diamond and an oval track is there for car and horse races. Courtesy of Reuel Griffin Collection, Archives, University of Alaska, Fairbanks

Possibly the May Queen contest about 1930 in the Empress Ballroom. Left to right are Marie Quick, Betty Hopkins, Helen Larsen, and Claire Weller. Courtesy of Frank Pettygrove Collection, Archives, University of Alaska, Fairbanks

The King and Queen Regent at the first Fairbanks Ice Carnival and Dog Derby in 1934. William Graigie and Catherine VanCurler reigned on an elaborate ice throne in fur garments.

The celebration was the brainchild of two young women, Mrs. Kay Hufman and Mrs. Clara Murray, who decided that a 1934 spring carnival would cheer up the community and allow young and old alike to celebrate the end of the winter. With the aid of Don Adler, manager of "Cap" Lathrop's Empress Theater, they started a publicity campaign, composed a song for the occasion, solicited the support of merchants and college and school officials, and staged the first Fairbanks Ice Carnival and Dog Derby. *Courtesy of Norma Hoyt Collection*

The Bentley dairy in the 1930s, near the present site of the Fred Meyers store. *Courtesy of Reuel Griffin Collection, Archives, University of Alaska, Fairbanks*

Mr. Kramer was a school janitor in 1933 at the temporary school building on Wickersham Street. Courtesy of Norma Hoyt Collection

The Moose Hall on Wickersham Street provided space for school classes after the school building burned in late 1932. It had long been a center for community activities, and in later years was converted to apartments and cold storage lockers. It was torn down in the 1960s. Note the icicles hanging from the eaves, a sign of poor insulation. Courtesy of Norma Hoyt Collection

The 1932 second grade on the steps of the old wooden public school. The original windows in the building had been replaced with larger ones. Courtesy of Norma Hoyt Collection

Main School was built of reinforced concrete to replace the old wooden school that burned in 1932. The central part was completed in 1934, the wings added later. Remodeled, it now serves as administrative headquarters for the school district. Courtesy of Reuel Griffin Collection, Archives, University of Alaska, Fairbanks

Norma C. Jordet (Hoyt) was a second grade teacher in the Fairbanks school in 1931. In Eskimo fur clothing, she is ready for the cold. She later continued her teaching career in Anchorage. Courtesy of Norma Hoyt Collection

The second grade in the spring of 1933 had to use temporary quarters in the Moose Hall until a new school could be built. The building on Wickersham Street had been one of the main gathering places for Fairbanksans for many years. Courtesy of Norma Hoyt Collection

The "Days of '98" were held by the American Legion in the 1930s. The chance to don fanciful costume was taken by this group. Left to right: Elizabeth Crites, Billy Miller, Bob Gleason, Lillian Crosson, Jim Crawford, Betty Spencer, Joe Crosson, and Cleora Bachner. Courtesy of Evolyn Melville Collection

Fairbanksans have always taken advantage of the rivers and forests that surround the town. Ed Clauson and Roy Furgeson on a camping trip about 1930 set up a comfortable camp along the banks of a small creek. Courtesy of Evolyn Melville Collection

The Fairbanks American Legion group presents
the keys to a new ambulance to city Major E. B.
Collins in the late 1930s. F. de la Vergne was a
local doctor at the time. Those identified are, left to
right: fourth, Frank Nash; fifth, John E. Youch,
Presbyterian minister; sixth, Dixie Hall;
seventh, Einar Tonseth (in the rear); eighth,
David Adler; eleventh, Mayor E. B. Collins;
twelfth, Alice Handley (face by windshield);
thirteenth, Mrs. Paul Mendel (behind Mrs.
Handley); fourteenth, Mrs. Collins (in dark
coat); (in the front row): fifteenth, Les Nerland (in
light coat); sixteenth, P. J. McDonald;
seventeenth, Ernie Shermer; eighteenth, Jack
Warren (in Legion cap).

Collins was mayor from 1934 to 1939. He
also mined, practiced law, served in the first
territorial legislature in 1913, and was a
delegate to the Alaska Constitutional Convention
held on the campus of the University of Alaska in
Fairbanks from November 1955 to April 1956.
Courtesy of Evolyn Melville Collection

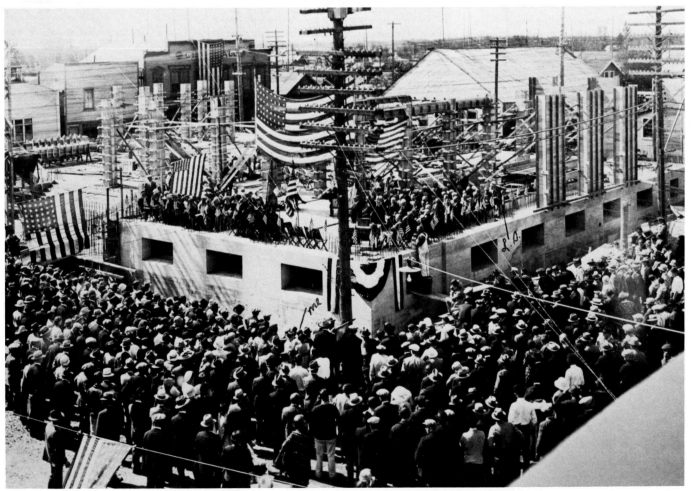

The laying of the cornerstone of the new Federal
Building, July 4, 1932. Dr Charles Bunnell of
the university was a principal speaker. This view
from the corner of First and Cushman looks
toward the old City Hall on Third Avenue.
Courtesy of Herbert Heller Collection, Archives,
University of Alaska, Fairbanks

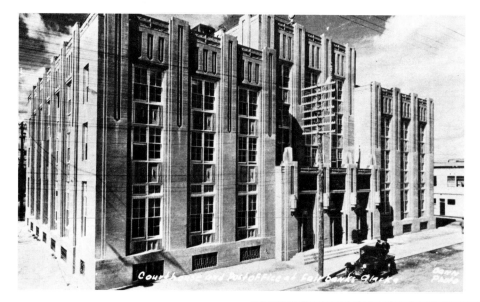

The Federal Building on Cushman Street with courthouse and post office functions was built in 1933-34. Although it no longer serves in its old role, the building has changed little from its original appearance. It was an imposing presence in a town that still consisted predominantly of log and small frame structures. *Courtesy of Reuel Griffin Collection, Archives, University of Alaska, Fairbanks*

The library above the gymnasium was built in 1935. In late November the 12,000 books in the library rooms of the main building were moved to their new quarters above the gymnasium. It took about thirteen hours to move the volumes. A staff of seven accomplished the task, and did so in an orderly fashion so that the books were shelved in their new quarters without confusion; in fact, the library remained open for business during the move. The University used this facility until the Bunnell Building with a new library was completed in 1960. A Sydney Laurence painting of Mt. McKinley is on the far wall. *Courtesy of Archives, University of Alaska, Fairbanks*

Genevieve Parker and her prize-winning dog team, about 1930, on the college campus. *Courtesy of Geist Collection, Archives, University of Alaska, Fairbanks*

The 1931-32 Alaska College of Agriculture and School of Mines Women's Basketball Team pose for a formal photograph. Left to right, standing: Jean Hunter Fowler, Helen Linck Atkinson (Frank), Claire Weller Whittaker, Violet Lundell O'Neill. Kneeling: Betty Scheffler Harrop, Audrey Steel, Ruby Olsen. Courtesy of Frank Pettygrove Collection, Archives, University of Alaska, Fairbanks

The college tumbling team in 1932-33. Left to right, seated: Alice Mikami, Hilja Reinikka, Audrey Steel, and Mary Mikami. Standing: Coach James C. Ryan, Beatrice Harkness, Tom Givan, Frank Pettygrove, Sidney Hendrickson, and Mildred Harkness. Ryan went on to become superintendent of schools in Fairbanks and commissioner of education. Ryan Junior High School is named after him. Courtesy of Frank Pettygrove Collection, Archives, University of Alaska, Fairbanks

A basketball game in the gymnasium at the university in 1936. Number 7 is Harry Lundell, near the pillar above him is Glen Franklin, and George Karabelnikoff is at the lower left corner. After the Patty Building was built, this gym was used as the University Museum until 1979. Courtesy of Helen L. Atkinson Collection

The college men's basketball team in 1932-33.
Left to right: Coach James C. Ryan, Don Fowler,
Harry Brandt, Paul Wickstrom, Tom Eck, Al
Dorsh, Bill O'Neil, and Dick Date. They are
standing outside the old gymnasium building.
Courtesy of Frank Pettygrove Collection,
Archives, University of Alaska, Fairbanks

Newsboys in front of the Fairbanks Daily News-Miner building at Third and Cushman, which was occupied until about 1935. From left to right: Don Raats, Claude St. Amand, Andy Growden, unidentified, Gary Simponen, John White, Bud Filson, Bill Growden, Bill Berry, Bob Jay, Don Agbaba, Stan Hanson, George _____, unidentified, L. St. Amand, Dave Tewksberry, Otis Berry, Tommy Olson, Steven Agbaba. Courtesy of William Waugaman

Second Avenue showing the beginning of change in the late 1930s. The Lathrop Building, housing the Fairbanks Daily News-Miner and the Lacey Street Theatre, stand among old false-fronts and frame business buildings. The small building at the left is the office of Lavery Airways. Courtesy of Reuel Griffin Collection, Archives, University of Alaska, Fairbanks

The Chamber of Commerce issued this map of the Fairbanks area in 1936. It shows Fairbanks in relation to the features of the surrounding countryside, and although the scale is distorted, the map still gives a good idea of places that were and that remain significant in the Fairbanks neighborhood. Courtesy of Helen L. Atkinson Collection

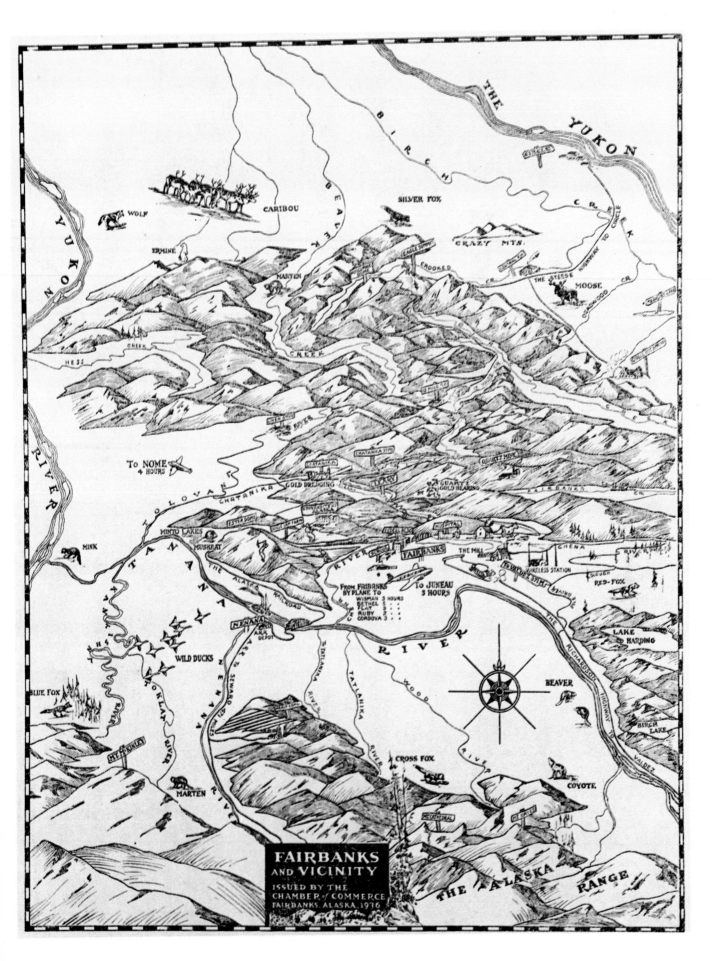

FAIRBANKS AND VICINITY

ISSUED BY THE CHAMBER of COMMERCE
FAIRBANKS, ALASKA, 1936

James Nordale and Mary Ann Link (Cole) posed on the porch of the old Link house on a warm summer day in 1935. The house with its screened porch and garden was on Second Avenue where the Doyon Building parking lot is now. Nordale went on to become borough attorney. Courtesy of Mathilde Link-Francine Mears Collection

The Link house on Second Avenue in 1934-35 was typical of the period. A large woodpile was necessary for the winter. Rain water was saved from the tin roof to use when the heavily iron-impregnated water from the tap could not be used for washing or cooking. The base of the house is built out and insulated to keep drafts and cold out. Frank Link splits the winter wood with a double-bitted ax while his daughter, Mary Ann, holds his cap and a ball. Courtesy of Mathilde Link-Francine Mears Collection

Mr. and Mrs. Link and Francine at 213 Dunkel Street, the house Frank Link built in 1938. Courtesy of Mathilde Link-Francine Mears Collection

Alice Hanley and Lou Kolbert, the Regents at the 1939 Ice Carnival. Mrs. Hanley's husband, William, had a plumbing and sheet metal shop on Seventh Avenue. Courtesy of Mathilde Link-Francine Mears Collection

The Fourth of July parade in 1935 and 1936 featured children's costumes. The bandaged child in the foreground is unidentified. Behind him with rabbit ears may be Mary Nordale. Katherine Nordale stands next to Mathilde Link, who holds her daughter Mary Ann's hand. Courtesy of Mathilde Link-Francine Mears Collection

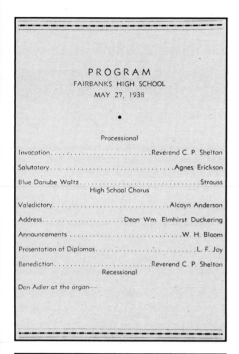

PROGRAM
FAIRBANKS HIGH SCHOOL
MAY 27, 1938

•

Processional

Invocation. . . . . .Reverend C. P. Shelton

Salutatory. . . . . .Agnes Erickson

Blue Danube Waltz. . . . . .Strauss
High School Chorus

Valedictory. . . . . .Alcoyn Anderson

Address. . . . . .Dean Wm. Elmhirst Duckering

Announcements . . . . .W. H. Bloom

Presentation of Diplomas. . . . . .L. F. Joy

Benediction. .Reverend C. P. Shelton
Recessional

Don Adler at the organ—

GRADUATING

Alcoyn Anderson
Virginia Mary Berry
Henry Warren Brewis
Betty Jean Buzby
Dan Francis Eagan
Agnes Alece Erickson
Dorothea Dell Geraghty
Shirley Bell Harkness
Patricia Hunter
Naimy Jackson
Helen Marlin
May Mayo
Emerelda Patrice McDonald
James Adair Miller
Ann Miscovich
Marion Dorothy Murphy
Nolan Phillips
Kenneth Paul Ringstad
Pierre St. Amand
Charles John Strandberg, Jr.
William George Stroecker

The program and graduate list from Fairbanks High School in 1938. Courtesy of Archives, University of Alaska, Fairbanks

Howard Hughes, on a round-the-world flight, stopped to refuel on July 13, 1938. Hughes, wearing the felt hat, is in the center of the group. The flight was made to promote the 1939 World's Fair in New York. Courtesy of C. L. Andrews Collection, Archives, University of Alaska, Fairbanks

A crowd gathered at Weeks Field for the arrival of the first air mail from Seattle to Fairbanks in 1936. The traveling time of the Pacific Alaska Airways plane was eighty hours. Walter Hall, the co-pilot, is in the door; postal serviceman Mr. Marsh is next to the right; then F. E Robins, the captain, in the pilot's cap. George Tuttle, the customs inspector, is to the right of the captain (without a hat). Courtesy of Norma Hoyt Collection

The Northern Commercial Company took over Barnette's trading post and joined the buildings along First Avenue to form one large store in 1903.

The Northern Commercial Company at once improved its new store with an addition, thirty by sixty feet, two stories high, of corrugated iron and building paper. It started to build a warehouse thirty by one-hundred feet with an eleven-foot ceiling to hold the winter's food for the camps. The big store promised a big camp, customers stated. The N. C. Company promoted Howard Turner from Circle on the Yukon River to manage the new branch on the Chena River. On March 15, 1905, Leon Sloss, the president of the company, appointed Volney Richmond to replace Turner,

who had resigned to go into a mining venture.

The building continued to look much the same until the 1950s. The windows were later boarded up, but as Nordstrom the building looks today much as it did in this 1920s photograph Courtesy of Craig Collection, Archives, University of Alaska, Fairbanks

Chapter III

WORLD WAR II AND THE POST-WAR YEARS

1941-1966

On December 7, 1941, the Japanese bombed Pearl Harbor and the United States was at war. In the next few years, the Army, Navy, and Civil Aeronautics Administration spent more than $400 million to build Alaska into a giant air base. At the end of the war, besides many other airports and two dozen auxiliary and intermediate fields, it had erected fifty-six radio ranges and sixty-six weather-reporting and communications stations, making instrument flight routine.

The war brought other monumental changes to Alaska. The territory now was recognized nationally as the "northern outpost" and the Interior as the strategic heartland of Alaska. The war, in fact, constituted a demarcation line between the seventy three years of American ownership of Alaska prior to 1940 and the forty one years since that time.

The transformation was rapid and dramatic. For more than a decade officials had been talking about a possible land link between Alaska and the States. In the spring of 1942 some 10,000 soldiers, divided into seven Army Engineer regiments and supported by 6,000 civilian workers under the direction of the United States Public Road Administration, started construction of the ALCAN (Alaska-Canadian Military Highway). Work began simultaneously at three locations: Dawson Creek, the terminal of a railroad running northwest from Edmonton, Alberta; at Whitehorse, Yukon Territory, which connected via the White Pass and Yukon Railway with Skagway on tidewater on the coast of southeastern Alaska; and at Big Delta in Alaska. The highway was completed with incredible speed, and in November of 1942 formally opened for traffic. The construction of 1,671 miles of road over formidable terrain had been an engineering feat of the first order. The cost of

The USO building, on the site of the old Nordale Hotel, has served the community and the military bases surrounding Fairbanks since World War II. Courtesy of Reuel Griffin Collection, Archives, University of Alaska, Fairbanks

construction amounted to approximately $135 million or $56,160 per mile, including the many bridges which cost approximately $23,166,725 to build.

Transportation, both commercial aviation and road travel, expanded, and capital expenditures for housing, heavy construction, community services, and other needs increased substantially. Most importantly, perhaps, the military returned to Alaska and to the Interior on a permanent basis, reflecting the territory's importance in the American defensive system.

During the war, and well into the 1960s, military activities dominated the local economy. Defense spending in the Fairbanks area averaged approximately $100 million per annum between 1940 and 1954. The 1950 census reported the city of Fairbanks as having 5,771 inhabitants, but not included in the count were 2,543 people in the following communities adjacent to and dependent upon the city:

College	425
Derby Tract	172
Ester	74
Garden Island	41
Hamilton Acres	214
Slaterville	611
Arctic Contractors	44
Eskimo	41
Fox	25
Graehl	476
Lemeta Tract	358
South Fairbanks	63

Adding the population of these areas to that of the city, the 1950 population of Fairbanks, excluding military and civilian personnel stationed on the two Air Force bases, amounted to 8,314 persons. Including the bases, the greater Fairbanks area had a population of 14,280, or 240 percent greater than in 1940.

Two major military installations exist in the Fairbanks area. When Congress appropriated $4 million in 1939, construction began of a cold-weather testing station for airplanes which was to be named Ladd Field. Construction began in 1940, and the first Army Air Corps detachment assigned to an Alaskan station arrived in Fairbanks on April 14, 1940. Ladd Field expanded rapidly during the war, providing employment for interior residents and newcomers alike at wages two or three times as high as they had ever enjoyed. During the 1950s major expansion took place, including construction of the $7.1 million Bassett military hospital. Eventually, the installation was renamed Fort Jonathan M. Wainwright and became an army base.

During the war, Ladd Field used a facility known as "Mile 26," some thirty miles south of Fairbanks, as a storage yard. In 1947 the installation was expanded and became a Strategic Air Command base. In February 1948 the Air Force honored aviation pioneer Carl Ben Eielson, naming the base for him. Jet interceptor aircraft and B-52 bombers are stationed at Eielson and make it the northernmost offensive base in the United States as well as the one closest to the Soviet Union.

In 1949 the Army chose Big Delta, some 100 miles south of the city, as the site of its new Arctic Indoctrination School and rapidly built Fort Greeley with its related airfield. And when the Korean War broke out in 1950, military activities increased, and funds for military construction doubled, tripled, and quadrupled.

The social and economic impact of these expenditures was great. Business boomed and provided hundreds of new retail and service needs which formerly could only be obtained Outside. Transportation and communications improved. Housing and community facilities were expanded and upgraded. This growth benefitted Fairbanks, but there were problems as well. Thousands of transient workers flocked to the city each summer to find high-paying

An improvement at Ladd Field was the completion of a 500-man barracks in 1949. Unmarried airmen lived here after formerly being hosued in Quonset huts. A second 500-men barracks was to be completed in 1950.

Ladd Field had been authorized in 1939. The first contingent of Air Corps personnel arrived in April 1940, headed by Major Dale C. Gaffney. The field was transferred to the U. S. Army in 1961 to become Fort Jonathan M. Wainwright. United States Air Force photo; courtesy of Fairbanks Daily News-Miner

jobs in the construction industry. With them, however, also came undesirable elements which thrive in boom conditions, and crime increased. In addition, the rapid expansion of the permanent population left city officials and planners struggling to cope with a myriad of problems and emergencies, such as housing and schools, recreational facilities, juvenile delinquency, utilities, police, fire protection, and inadequate medical facilities, to name a few.

In short, the war drastically changed Alaska's population, economy, and social structure. More than 300,000 servicemen were stationed in Alaska between 1941 and 1945, while the territory's population increased from 72,524 in 1940 to 128,643 by 1950, or by 77.4 percent. The Interior registered a 122.4 percent increase between 1940 and 1950, second only to the southcentral region with Anchorage as the focal point which grew by an astounding 236.6 percent. In a twenty-eight year period, between 1940 and 1968, the figures are even more striking. In 1940 Alaska had a total military population of about 1,000 in a civilian population of 72,524. By 1968 the military residents, including dependents and civilian Department of Defense personnel, totaled 79,000 in a civilian population of 279,000.

The economic impact of the military remained a substantial feature of post-war Alaska well into the 1960s. The following figures reveal just how important the military was. In 1954, the military percentage of total employment in Alaska amounted to 47 percent—but only 5 percent in the contiguous states. By 1960, the military percentage of total employment had slipped to 33.3 percent, and amounted to only 4 percent in the contiguous states.

At the end of the war, over 300 major and minor military installations had been built in the north, costing several billion dollars. Today, nine major and fifty four smaller installations remain. And although troop levels declined sharply in the post-war period, from 60,000 in 1945 to 26,000 in 1950, they rose again because of the start of the Korean War. Military personnel reached a peak of 50,000 in 1955 and then slowly declined to 33,000 in 1970.

Communities with military bases benefitted from funds spent for construction, operations, maintenance, and military and civilian wage disbursements. Between 1960 and 1969 total military expenditures averaged $238.4 million per year. The United States Army Corps of Engineers spent another $42 million during this ten year period. By 1968, estimates placed military capital investment in Alaska at $2.1 billion, not including land values. Between 1959 and 1969, the Department of Defense spent $3,523,000,000, six times as much as any other federal agency.

In 1960, out of Alaska's total employed labor force, some 56 percent worked for federal, state, or local governmental bodies, and the private sector employed only 44 percent. In the interior the various governmental agencies employed 66.4 percent of the labor force. This compares to a 15.9 percent government employment level for the United States in 1960 and reflects Alaska's reliance on governmental expenditures.

The military, however, has also had a social influence because of its diverse role and participation in non-military support activities. For example, the military participates in the construction and clearing of roads and recreation trails, builds shelter cabins, surveys and protects wildlife, undertakes search and rescue missions, and provides medical assistance when needed. In short, in addition to its combat responsibilities, the military has become an economic, political, and social asset, lending stability to society in the Interior.

Above all, the war activities swept away most vestiges of the old Fairbanks, which had been a closely knit community. While some bemoaned the fading of the old, many others maintained that military spending had rescued a town struggling to survive and transformed it into a modern urban center.

Still another change of momentous consequence occurred in 1958. After a struggle for self-government which had started in earnest in 1944, Congress finally passed a statehood measure in 1958. The United States Senate approved the measure on June 30, 1958, at 8:02 P.M. Eastern Standard Time. Word flashed back to Alaska almost immedi-

ately, and residents began to celebrate. The *Fairbanks Daily News-Miner* prepared a special statehood edition and rushed copies to the nation's capital in time for every member of Congress to have a copy on his desk on July First. C. W. "Bill" Snedden, the publisher of the paper, intended to demonstrate to Congress how close the forty ninth state really was in the age of modern transportation. Fairbanks residents lit bonfires, and a chemical was dumped into the Chena

River to change its color to gold—a trick which did not quite come off. Bars did a booming business, and the majority of Alaskans welcomed their new political status. On January 3, 1959, President Dwight D. Eisenhower signed the proclamation which officially admitted Alaska into the Union of States as the forty-ninth state. A new era had begun for Alaska.

Second Avenue looking west from Lacey Street in the late 1940s. The N. C. Power Plant stacks were still standing. Courtesy of Craig Collection, Archives, University of Alaska, Fairbanks

Armed Forces Day, May 18, 1953, brought ther army with its equipment to Second Avenue. The military presence in Fairbanks had become important economically and socially with World War II, and nearby bases have continued to be an asset to the community. Courtesy of Reuel Griffin Collection, Archives, University of Alaska, Fairbanks

The N. C. Company board transferred the telephone system to the City Hall in 1947. Here, the new telephone cable is being laid in mid-November near the N. C. power plant. Courtesy of Reuel Griffin Collection, Archives, University of Alaska, Fairbanks

At the installation of the new telephone switchboard on December 20, 1947 were, left to right: unidentified, Bernie Carr, and Hjalmar Nordale.

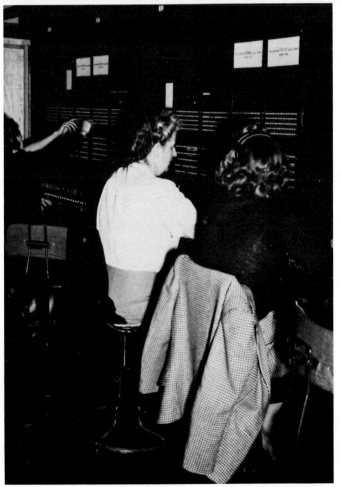

The telephone switchboard in the late 1940s. Bertha Downing is the operator in the center. Courtesy of Reuel Griffin Collection, Archives, University of Alaska, Fairbanks

The third and fourth grades of the Immaculate Conception School in the basement of the Catholic Church, 1947. This was the first year the school was in operation. In the picture are, left to right, first row: Buzz Young, Raymond Holmstrom, Terry Papovich, Patty Orsini, Mike Cook, Duane Mattis, Jenny Doheney, Pat McFaddin, Sherwood Mathis, and Raymond Young. Second row: John Nielson, Diane Kidman, Sue Schloefeldt, "the unidentified twins," unidentified, and Wilda Balke. third row: unidentified, unidentified, Darleen De Wree, Francine Link, Barbara Sellars, and Sister Joan of the Sisters of Providence. Top row: Joey Burns, Jim Sellars, Denny Krize, and unidentified. Courtesy of Mathilde Link-Francine Mears Collection

The Wien Brothers in 1946. (Left to right): Fritz, Noel and Sigurd standing beside a Wien Airlines Boeing 247. The Wiens are a significant factor in the development of aviation in Alaska and today Wien Air Alaska continues to serve the state. Courtesy of Archives, University of Alaska, Fairbanks

John and Edith Holm and their sons James (left) and Stuart perhaps typify the many individuals who came to Alaska after World War II to make their homes and establish their families. The Holms homesteaded on the Chena Hot Springs road and farmed for thirteen years. In 1959 they opened a landscaping and garden supply business. Both were involved in civic organizations and state political activities. John served in the state House of Representatives in 1963-65 and again from 1967 to 1973. This photo was taken at their homestead in 1947. Courtesy of John and Edith Holm

The 4H Potato Club at the Agricultural Experiment Station in College in 1943. The group is learning to sort potatoes, still a valuable crop in Interior Alaska. Courtesy of Mathilde Link-Francine Mears Collection

Their 1944 calendar showed that Nerlands brought the latest up-to-date and fashionable home furnishings to Interior Alaska. Courtesy of William Waugaman

Ready to Do More Than Its Part

One title for this eye-pleasing room might be "The Maidless Kitchen." But whether you are doing without a maid for the first time, or are one of the millions of busy homemakers who are now busier than ever—you can appreciate its many work-saving, time-saving features. Notice all the little things planned to save just as many steps, motions, and minutes as possible. Take the combination cart-breakfast table, for example, or the homemaker's desk in the corner. And don't overlook the smart Armstrong's Linoleum Floor—that will save many hours that are too valuable these days to spend on floor cleaning.

ANDREW NERLAND
LINOLEUM

FURNITURE   RUGS

INTERIOR DECORATING
FAIRBANKS, ALASKA

			JANUARY			1944			FEBRUARY			
Sun.	Mon.	Tue.	Wed.	Thu.	Fri.	Sat.	Sun.	Mon.	Tue.	Wed.	Thu.	Fri.	Sat.
						1			1	2	3	4	5
2	3	4	5	6	7	8	6	7	8	9	10	11	12
9	10	11	12	13	14	15	13	14	15	16	17	18	19
16	17	18	19	20	21	22	20	21	22	23	24	25	26
23/30	24/31	25	26	27	28	29	27	28	29				

ARMSTRONG'S LINOLEUM FLOORS FOR EVERY ROOM IN THE HOUSE

The fire of January 4, 1946, destroyed much of the south side of Second Avenue, just west of Cushman. All the present buildings in this area were built after this fire. Courtesy of Reuel Griffin Collection, Archives, University of Alaska, Fairbanks

Virginia Sparling and Elizabeth Crites (Bradford), graduates of the University of Alaska class of 1945, stood outside the north door of the old gymnasium-library-museum building with Austin E. Lathrop, then vice-president of the Board of Regents. Courtesy of Virginia Verle Sparling

Some of the university regents in the 1940s were, left to right: Tom Donohue, J. W. Gibson, Harriet Hess, A. E. "Cap" Lathrop, and Andrew Nerland. Courtesy of William Cashen Collection, Archives, University of Alaska, Fairbanks

Opposite Page:
Ed Hoch, Vince Magnuson, and Ben Atkinson clean their catch along the banks of the Salcha River in the late 1940s. The Salcha and other rivers around Fairbanks provide continuing recreational opportunities for fishermen, hunters, and boaters. Courtesy of Helen L. Atkinson Collection

Banding beaver pelts in front of Kayes Store on Second Avenue in the late 1940s. The sign over the window advertises "Military Supplies, insignias, and chevrons." Fur trapping was still important in the Interior, and many furs came through Fairbanks. Courtesy of Reuel Griffin Collection, Archives, University of Alaska, Fairbanks

A party at the Eagles Hall in 1948 included many Fairbanks women, some in rather odd hats. Seated in the front row from the left are Mrs. Love (first president of the Eagles Auxiliary), Gladys Peterson, Myrtle Pratt, Sally Conora, Rachel Wright, and Elizabeth Hubbard. Kathy Fulton is in a dark dress behind Sally Conora; next to her is Beth Rust in a white blouse; at her right is Barbara Lindberg. Laura Wright holds black purse in the center of the photo. Billie Jukow is behind the woman with the doll on her head, while Ann Backner, Mrs. Jackovich, and Lila Grant are at the end of that row. Marge Lockwood, Alice Stryken, and Mrs. Cassady are also in the group. Courtesy of Mathilde Link-Francine Mears Collection

The Winter Carnival stage on the Chena River ice in 1949. The back of the old hospital shows at the upper left. Courtesy of Mathilde Link-Francine Mears Collection

The Ice Carnival in 1949 featured a parade on Second Avenue. Blanchfield Alley ran between the Black and White Liquor Store and Piggly Wiggly (later Coopers Hardware). The alley and the space occupied by the building between it and the Lathrop Building are now a city parking lot. Courtesy of Mathilde Link-Francine Mears Collection

Dog races continued on the river until the 1940s. The crowds lined the bridge and the riverbank to watch their favorite teams. Courtesy of Reuel Griffin Collection, Archives, University of Alaska, Fairbanks

One impressive Ice Carnival event is the Eskimo blanket toss. A walrus skin, ringed by volunteers, is used like a trampoline to send the jumper high into the air. This carnival took place in the late 1940s. Courtesy of Reuel Griffin Collection, Archives, University of Alaska, Fairbanks

The "mutt" parade at the 1948 or 1949 Winter Ice Carnival. Children costumed their pets and led them before the judges and appreciative neighbors. Courtesy of Mathilde Link-Francine Mears Collection

The KFAR transmitter on Farmer's Loop Road was built about 1940. The station was established by "Cap" Lathrop in 1939 and could be received through much of the Interior. A popular program was Tundra Topics, which carried private messages to isolated villages, miners, and trappers. Courtesy of Reuel Griffin Collection, Archives, University of Alaska, Fairbanks

The privately owned pool on Wendell Street was a summer favorite with all the kids in town in the late 1940s. Season tickets were available. Courtesy of Mathilde Link-Francine Mears Collection

Augie Hiebert on the early KFAR staff announced children's birthdays with the help of his dog "Sparky," who barked at the appropriate time. Hiebert came to Fairbanks when the station was started by "Cap" Lathrop in 1939. Courtesy of Reuel Griffin Collection, Archives, University of Alaska, Fairbanks

Maury Smith, the hometown reporter for many years on KFAR, is shown in 1958. Smith not only was known in the community for his news broadcasts but also was a familiar sight on Fairbanks streets on his bicycle long before their present popularity. *Courtesy of* Fairbanks Daily News-Miner

In 1953 the KFAR staff sent out this Christmas card to their friends and listeners. KFAR, founded in 1939, had offices in the Lathrop Building as well as a transmitter on Farmer's Loop Road. Several staff members went on to distinguished careers in broadcasting in Alaska and the Pacific Northwest. *Courtesy of Mathilde Link-Francine Mears Collection*

Fairview Manor, a new housing complex in Fairbanks, was built to meet the need of military families and construction workers who came to Fairbanks with World War II. It was first occupied in 1951. Airport Road and Cowles street meet in the lower right. *Courtesy of Reuel Griffin Collection, Archives, University of Alaska, Fairbanks*

A Rotary Club luncheon at the North Pole Bakery in the 1940s. Phil Johnson is at the left (with dark hair); Bob Brandt is in the center foreground. Courtesy of Reuel Griffin Collection, Archives, University of Alaska, Fairbanks

Mary Ann Link in the Empress Theatre box office in 1949. The staff wore uniforms, and the box office featured leaded and cut glass. The admission prices, sixty cents for adults and twenty cents for children, are only a fond memory today. Courtesy of Mathilde Link-Francine Mears Collection

Cushman Street in 1949 looking south from the bridge. Cushman Street was paved but First Avenue was not. Courtesy of Reuel Griffin Collection, Archives, University of Alaska, Fairbanks

ST. — FAIRBANKS, ALASKA

The First National Bank in 1947 or 1948. Included in the picture are, left to right: Gladys Conradt, Jim McClung (behind counter), Edward H. Stroecker, Jean Niemi, Frank DeWree, Millie Brandt, William Stroecker, Edward F. Stroecker, and Ben McFarland. Sam Bonnifield started the bank in 1905 and Luther Hess was associated with it from 1905 to 1918. Edward F. Stroecker went to work for the bank as a teller and became president in 1929. William Stroecker began as a bookkeeper in 1947, was elected to the board of directors in 1954, and became president in 1965. After he sold his interest in 1977, he became chairman of the board of Alaska Pacific Bank Corporation. Courtesy of Reuel Griffin Collection, Archives, University of Alaska, Fairbanks

Samson's Hardware started in early Fairbanks and continues in the same location and in the same style today. This interior view taken in 1948 could have been taken thirty years earlier or later. Courtesy of Reuel Griffin Collection, Archives, University of Alaska, Fairbanks

Gordon's Store in one of the older buildings in Fairbanks on Cushman between Third and Fourth in 1948 closed after the 1967 flood. It specialized in ladies' wear and dry goods. Courtesy of Reuel Griffin Collection, Archives, University of Alaska, Fairbanks

John Butrovich talks to the office staff at the Alaska Insurance Company. Born in 1910 at Fairbanks Creek, a mining camp 26 miles north of the city, Butrovich graduated from Fairbanks High School in 1929 and established the Alaska Insurance Company in 1936. After being a city councilman and utilities board member in Fairbanks he served in the territorial Senate from 1945 to 1957 and the state Senate from 1963 to 1979. A room in the state capitol is named in his honor. Courtesy of Reuel Griffin Collection, Archives, University of Alaska, Fairbanks

The Arctic Alaska Travel Service, founded by Chuck West, behind the counter, eventually grew into Westours, a major travel service in the western United States. Courtesy of Reuel Griffin Collection, Archives, University of Alaska, Fairbanks

The Model Cafe was the most popular eating place in town into the 1950s. This is a 1948 view. Courtesy of Reuel Griffin Collection, Archives, University of Alaska, Fairbanks

The Standard Garage and the University Bus Lines, with Paul Greiman as proprietor, were located at the corner of Second and Noble in 1948. Courtesy of Reuel Griffin Collection, Archives, University of Alaska, Fairbanks

Ernest F. Jessen (left), who worked briefly with the Fairbanks Daily News-Miner in the early 1940s, started his own Jessen's Weekly, which evolved into the still published All-Alaska Weekly. Courtesy of Reuel Griffin Collection, Archives, University of Alaska, Fairbanks

The North Pole Bakery on Second Avenue was a popular spot for baked goods in the 1940s. It had been a fixture for many years along the main shopping street in the city. Drug stores, meat markets, newsands, groceries, and clothiers along Second Avenue provided for a family's needs in the center of town. Courtesy of Reuel Griffin Collection, Archives, University of Alaska, Fairbanks

Cooper's Hardware was located on Second Avenue in the 1940s. It provided not only basic hardware needs but housewares as well. Courtesy of Reuel Griffin Collection, Archives, University of Alaska, Fairbanks

Piggly-Wiggly in the 1940s was a supermarket that showed the transition from the traditional grocery store to the large modern foodstores. The open shelves and the central checkout area were innovations. The store was later located on Gaffney Road. Courtesy of Reuel Griffin Collection, Archives, University of Alaska, Fairbanks

Frank Link and Ed Schone at the Link Shop, 301 Second Avenue. They were among the many entrepreneurs who established small businesses to serve the needs of the self-contained town in the 1930s and 1940s. Courtesy of Mathilde Link-Francine Mears Collection

Curling in the early 1950s in the original rink on Second Avenue. In 1962 a new rink with six sheets of ice was built. It now has artificial ice. Harry Avakoff, an avid curler and a skip for forty seven years, has just sent a stone down the ice in this picture. Pete Peterson is at the right. Courtesy of Reuel Griffin Collection, Archives, University of Alaska, Fairbanks

Fire continued to be a hazard in Fairbanks. When it happened in the winter, as in 1946, the ice that formed as the water froze could create its own dangers and make salvage difficult. Courtesy of Mathilde Link-Francine Mears Collection

Twenty-nine pioneers gathered for the 1948 Ice Carnival. All those pictured came to Alaska before or during 1898.

Left to right, front row: George Roberts, John Conte, Matt Taipole, Henry Appelle, Lawrence Olson, Olie W. Fisher, Anton Bahke. Second row: Thomas J. J. Buckley, Thomas W. Pearson, Richard C. Rothenburg.

Third row: "Shortie" Wallace, Charles Knutson, Al Young, Frank Young, Joseph Oates, Max Manger, Charles Crawford. Fourth row: W. W. Hunter, Erick Nelson, Ole Berg, Peter Coulombe, William Behan, Martin Pinska, Charles Lynn, John Vik. Courtesy of Historical Photograph Collection, Archives, University of Alaska, Fairbanks

The new American Legion Hall, now the Presbyterian Hospitality House, was dedicated about 1954. At the ceremony were, left to right: Einar Tonseth, unidentified, Reverend Bingle, unidentified, and Forbes Baker, head of the post at that time. The building on Airport Road near Fairview Manor became the Presbyterian Hospitality House in 1957. Courtesy of Evolyn Melville Collection

A small band for a local wedding. The reception for Pat and Joe Lawlor's wedding, about 1955, was held at the Tanana Valley Sportsman Association Lodge. In the group were Edith Holm, Harold Downing, Downing's son-in-law, Louis Johnson, Betty Dirgen, and Bert Dirgen. The informality was reminiscent of earlier scenes when new groups came to make homes on the frontier. Courtesy of John and Edith Holm

A group at the Eagles Hall in the 1950s. Seated, from left to right: Mary Stock, Kathy Fulton, Dorothy Johnson, Virginia Johnson, Dorothea Collins, unidentified, Tillie Link. Second row: unidentified, Betty Kjera, Myrtle Ostby. Marvin Ostby, unidentified, unidentified, unidentified, Eugene Brazeau. Third row: unidentified, Mr. Love, Ed Kjera, unidentified, unidentified, unidentified, and John Carlson. Courtesy of Mathilde Link-Francine Mears Collection

The Ice Carnival in 1950 was held on the river. Left to right: Queen Maxine Cothern, King Regent Arthur Lutro, unidentified, and manager "Storing" Shideler. Polar bear rugs are on the ice throne behind them. Mrs. Welmer was Queen Regent. Courtesy of Mathilde Link-Francine, Mears Collection

The Northward Building, under construction in 1951, is one of Fairbanks's "skyscrapers." Used as a model for the "ice palace" of Edna Ferber's novel, it continues to house apartments, offices, and businesses such as the Alaska National Bank. Courtesy of Reuel Griffin Collection, Archives, University of Alaska, Fairbanks

Frank P. Young and Henry Appele posed together in July 1957. Young came north in 1896 and Appele, who was ninety years old at the time the picture was taken, came north in 1894. Young still resides in Fairbanks. Both were members of the Pioneers of Alaska, Igloo No. 4. *Courtesy of* Fairbanks Daily News-Miner

Edith Holm shot a lynx at her homestead door in 1957. Life on a new homestead could be rough even in the mid-twentieth century. Long hours and hard work were just as vital to success as they had been in early Fairbanks. *Courtesy of John and Edith Holm*

An aerial view in the 1950s shows how the town has grown into a city with development on both banks of the Chena River. Courtesy of Herbert Heller Collection, Archives, University of Alaska, Fairbanks

The Pioneer Hotel, one of the old landmarks, burned on July 15, 1952. It had expanded over the years into several buildings but was notable for the long stretch of bay windows on the second floor. Courtesy of Reuel Griffin Collection, Archives, University of Alaska, Fairbanks

The Chena River could still be used by float planes near town in the 1940s. The plane nearest the bridge belongs to Wien Alaska Airways, Inc. Courtesy of Reuel Griffin Collection, Archives, University of Alaska, Fairbanks

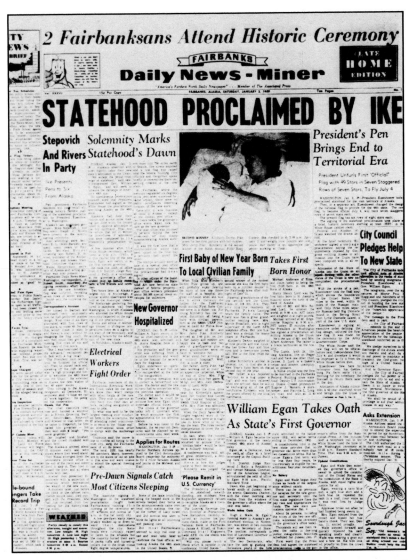

The Fairbanks Daily News-Miner of
January 3, 1959, carried news of the statehood
proclamation. For most Alaskans, the big day
had come the previous June when Congress had
passed the statehood act. Courtesy of Archives,
University of Alaska, Fairbanks

The Fairbanks International Airport was
constructed in 1949-51 to replace Weeks Field.
This early view shows none of the terminal and
hangar complexes that would be developed near
the newly completed runways. The Tanana River
is to the left. Courtesy of Reuel Griffin Collection,
Archives, University of Alaska, Fairbanks

149

A "49th" star is to be raised to celebrate statehood. This scene is possibly on top of the Lathrop Building. Courtesy of Fairbanks Daily News-Miner

The Constitutional Convention met at the University of Alaska on November 8, 1955 to draft a constitution for the proposed state. This bold group labored for seventy-four days and then posed after their effort and signed the photograph. Courtesy of Archives, University of Alaska, Fairbanks

In the early 1950s the road on Garden Island still made a sharp bend around the St. Joseph's Hospital complex. The old wing of the hospital was still standing, as was the old railroad depot in the left foreground. Courtesy of Archives, University of Alaska, Fairbanks

A cold spell during the 1961 Christmas season produced this series of headlines in the Fairbanks Daily News-Miner. Coping with the cold was everyone's first priority. The Municipal Utility System and Golden Valley Electric Association both were powered with coal brought from Healy by the Alaska Railroad. Their power was needed for lighting and to keep home heating systems going during this dark part of the year. Courtesy of Fairbanks Daily News-Miner

A 1962 Christmas party at the Masonic Temple at the regular meeting of the Midnight Sun Chapter No. 6 O.E.S. brought together many longtime Fairbanksans. In the group are, left to right, seated: Lola Colette, Helen Bell, Ester Ward, Hertha Baker, Ruth Barrack, and Lucille Meath. Standing: Francis Erickson, Grover McCarty, Margaret Lee, Jens Jorgenson, Mariel Wilbur, Pearl Scherer, Mildred Nerland (hidden), Annella Davis, Elizabeth Crites Bradford, and Dorothy Pattinson. Courtesy of Evolyn Melville Collection

The Fairbanks area is cleaned up by volunteers every spring. Here a young group in 1963 picks up litter along College Road. Courtesy of Evolyn Melville Collection

Sam White was a pioneer game warden and bush pilot in Alaska. He first came north in 1922 and became a game warden for the new Alaska Game Commission in 1927. The Wiens taught him to fly, and he was the first to use a plane in game warden work. In 1941 he became a bush pilot, working for Noel Wien out of Anchorage, and continued bush flying until his retirement at age seventy in 1962 in Fairbanks. Courtesy of Archives, University of Alaska, Fairbanks

The Barnette House on First Avenue was torn down in the 1960s. Only the names of a street and a school remain to remind us of the founder of Fairbanks. Courtesy of Harrie Hughes Collection, Archives, University of Alaska, Fairbanks

Construction on the main building on campus started in 1918. Finished in 1925, it was the principal classroom building until it was torn down in 1960. For years it symbolized the growth of the university under Dr. Charles Bunnell. Memorial Plaza occupies the site of the main building now. Courtesy of George Soli Collection, Archives, University of Alaska, Fairbanks

The University of Alaska Presidential Inaugural Dinner, October 23, 1960. Dr. Ernest M. Patty, outgoing president of the university, is at the lectern. At the table are, left to right: Elmer Rasmuson, Mrs. William Egan, and the new president, Dr. William R. Wood. Courtesy of Archives, University of Alaska, Fairbanks

Ivar Skarland, who graduated from the college in 1935, went on to earn a Ph.D. at Harvard then returned to teach anthropology and head the Museum for many years. An active crosscountry skier during his college days, he continued as a skier until his death in 1970. Courtesy of Joseph Fejes Collection, Archives, University of Alaska, Fairbanks

A University of Alaska faculty party in the 1960s at the Malemute Saloon in Ester. At the front table are Charles K. Ray and William R. Cashen. Pounding the bar is Earl Beistline, and leaning on it is Colonel Kenneth C. Haycraft.

Betty Lister and Ivar Skarland watch the proceedings from the right. Courtesy of Ivar Skarland Collection, Archives, University of Alaska, Fairbanks

In 1926, Otto Wm. Geist, a German immigrant affiliated with the Alaska Agricultural College and School of Mines, conducted a reconnaissance trip to St. Lawrence Island. The archeological and ethnological specimens he brought back that year warranted active research in this field. Lacking other financial support, Dr. Charles E. Bunnell, president of the College, and Geist carried on the work as the Bunnell-Geist Bering Sea Expeditions.

By 1930 much work had been accomplished, and the territorial legislature, alerted to the importance of continuing the work, appropriated money to carry on the Alaska College Expedition to St. Lawrence Island. As a result the College Museum came into possession of a comprehensive collection of Alaska Eskimo artifacts.

In the summer of 1934 Geist, as the archeologist in charge, supervised a group of seven who excavated the ancient village site of Kukulik, near Savoonga on the north coast of St. Lawrence Island. Here they found objects of the so-called Punuk and old Bering Sea cultures. The results of this work appeared in 1936 in a volume entitled Archaeological Excavations at Kukulik, co-authored by Geist and Froehlich G. Rainey. In 1935 Geist officially became a staff member of the University. For many years he collected fossils from the gold operations in the Fairbanks region under a contract with the Frick Laboratories of the American Museum of Natural History and the University of Alaska. Courtesy of William Cashen Collection, Archives, University of Alaska, Fairbanks

Dr. William R. Wood, president of the University of Alaska, examines some of the gold coins and objects which Mr. and Mrs. Robert Bloom donated to the University Museum in 1968. Jessie Bloom helped to organize the Girl Scouts in Fairbanks. Robert Bloom was one of the early regents of the college. Courtesy of University of Alaska Museum

The charter members of the Fairbanks Frontier Chapter of the Sweet Adelines, a "barbershop" singing group, posed in April 1966. Left to right, first row: Del Pruhs, Ruby Riddle, Maxine Meyers, Kitty Siebels, Pat Greuel, Gen Sole (director), Flo Cameron, Vera Heilman, Mary Brown, and Charlene Mantary. Second row: Christine Buck, Elaine Jacobson, Elly Downes, Edith Holm, Karen McElroy, Linda Klein, Ev Thye, Nancy Backner, and Roberta Bulstrode. Third row: Helen Weitz, Lillian Gotchell, Jan Walker, Sue Roberts, Joan Lauderbock, Luane Spake, and Tony Kitze. Courtesy of John and Edith Holm

New officers were installed at an annual meeting of the Fairbanks Chapter of the American Red Cross in August 1966. From left, seated: Barbara Trigg, secretary; Adrianna Coyle, second vice chairman; Sylvia Ringstad, vice chairman; Irene Brooks, board member. Standing: Clair Lammers, board member; Fred Randall, treasurer; John Murphy, board member; Leonard Lobban, chapter chairman; and Edward Wagner, outgoing chairman. Lobban and Murphy received five year service pins during the meeting. Courtesy of Fairbanks Daily News-Miner

MAY WE SUGGEST

FAIRBANKS No 1	. . .	$0.75
FAIRBANKS No 2	. . .	.75
ALASKA COCKTAIL	. . .	.75
GOLFERS DELIGHT	. . .	.75
COUNTRY CLUB COOLER	. . .	.75
GOLDEN NORTH RICKEY	. . .	.75
CHEECHAKO HI-BALL	. . .	.75
PLACERS PUNCH	. . .	.85
FORTYNINTH STAR	. . .	.85
YUKON SPECIAL	. . .	.85
GLACIER DRIP	. . .	1.00
FARTHEST NORTH FLIP	. . .	1.00
MIDNIGHT SUN SOUR	. . .	1.00
BEDROCK PUNCH	. . .	1.00
MUSHERS TODDY	. . .	1.00
AURORA BOREALIS	. . .	1.00
LAST FRONTIER FIZZ	. . .	1.25
CARIBOU COBBLER	. . .	1.25
NUGGET (KING SIZE)	. . .	1.25
IGLOO ICER	. . .	1.25
SOURDOUGHS DREAM	. . .	1.50
MOOSE MILK	. . .	1.50

The bar card from the Fairbanks Golf and Country Club in the early 1940s offered some exotic concoctions. Courtesy of Archives, University of Alaska, Fairbanks.

Eva McGown at one of her famous teas, serving a group of admirers. Courtesy of Reuel Griffin Collection, Archives, University of Alaska, Fairbanks

This view in June 1966 shows the beginning of construction on the J. C. Penney building. The 80,900 square foot building was a major commitment by a national chain to the community. *Courtesy of* Fairbanks Daily News-Miner

Ruth Forbes, who was very active in supporting and promoting music and arts activities in Fairbanks, hosted a theatre party in May 1966 at the Lacey Street Theatre with a special showing of My Fair Lady. *A hat competition was held. Left to right: Connie Ost, Mrs. Forbes, Delores Dodson, and Penny Eskridge. Courtesy of* Fairbanks Daily News-Miner

Officers of the Lodge, Eagles Auxiliary No. 1037, in June 1965. The first row from left to right includes: Fay Tyles, Tillie Link, Dina Wells, Fran Martindale, Freda Baumeister, Clara Johnson, and Dorothy Johnson. In the second row are: Dorothea Collins, unidentified, Rita Kraus, Mona Johnson, Mary Stock, and Jessie Anderson. Courtesy of Mathilde Link-Francine Mears Collection

This small engine, supposedly the first used by the Tanana Valley Railroad, was exhibited near the depot until 1966 when it was moved to the A-67 site, now Alaskaland.

The building to the left was moved from the town of Chena and operated near the depot as a restaurant for a number of years in the mid-1920s. The building now has an overhang over the first floor that was added after this photo was taken. Courtesy of Reuel Griffin Collection, Archives, University of Alaska, Fairbanks

surrounded by growing suburbs, the refuge is an interesting addition to the city and is used by school classes and visitors. Courtesy of Reuel Griffin Collection, Archives, University of Alaska, Fairbanks

Chapter IV

THE OIL YEARS

1967-1981

In August 1967, disaster struck the town. The Chena River, which bisects Fairbanks, overflowed its banks and put much of the city under some eight feet of water. Property damage was heavy, but fortunately the federal government quickly lent a helping hand. The Small Business Administration extended necessary long-term loans at favorable rates of interest to put Fairbanks back on its feet.

Early in 1968 Alaskans perked their ears when Atlantic-Richfield Company struck the ten-billion barrel Prudhoe Bay oilfield on the North Slope. In the subsequent oil lease sale in 1969, the twenty-third since Alaska had been admitted as the forty-ninth state to the Union in 1959, oil companies bid in excess of $900 million. Euphoria reigned, and there was hope that Alaska's perpetually rocky economy would now stabilize and diversify.

The oil would have to be hauled out, and the companies selected an 800-mile route from Prudhoe Bay via Fairbanks to tidewater at Valdez. The Trans-Alaska Pipeline System (TAPS), an unincorporated joint venture of Atlantic-Richfield, British Petroleum, and Humble Oil, applied to the United States Department of the Interior in June 1969 for a permit to construct a hot-oil pipeline across the 800 miles of public domain from Prudhoe Bay to Valdez. TAPS estimated that it would cost approximately $900 million to build the pipeline. In anticipation of immediate construction, many Fairbanks businesses laid in large inventories and made long-term financial commitments. Innumerable delays intervened, however, and it was not until January 23, 1974, that the secretary of the interior signed the primary federal right-of-way permit for construction of the Trans-Alaska Pipeline. In the meantime, many of the Fairbanks businesses which had made preparations for the boom experienced bankruptcies, and others underwent drastic financial reorganization.

By the summer of 1974, however, construction began in earnest. TAPS had metamorphosed into the

The Hering Auditorium at Lathrop High School was a refuge for many during the '67 flood. Many public buildings were made available to house the displaced. Cars were moved to high ground to protect them, and many people were able to save their possessions; others, however, were caught unaware of the impending flood and lost everything. Courtesy of D. Johnson Collection, Archives, University of Alaska, Fairbanks

The All-America City Award sponsored by the National Municipal League and Look Magazine was awarded to Fairbanks in 1968 in recognition of the effort and success of the community in overcoming the damage and setbacks of the 1967 flood. Courtesy of the City of Fairbanks

1968
ALL-AMERICA CITY
AWARD

Presented to

FAIRBANKS

in recognition of progress achieved through intelligent citizen action

AWARD JURY

AWARD SPONSORS
National Municipal League and Look Magazine

tightly organized Alyeska Pipeline Service Company, Inc., and coordinated the effort. The magnitude of the project was truly overwhelming. First, a 361-mile long gravel road would be built from the Yukon River to Prudhoe Bay, including bridges over twenty major streams and rivers and the construction of a 2,300-foot bridge over the Yukon River. Other preliminary construction included three permanent and eight temporary airfields, fifteen permanent and numerous temporary access roads, and nineteen construction camps. The second phase of the project, to be completed by mid-1977, included laying of a 798-mile-long, 48-inch diameter steel pipeline from Prudhoe Bay to Valdez, part of the pipe buried and part of it elevated above the ground. The final stage included construction of four additional pump stations and more oil storage and tanker docking facilities at Valdez. The whole project was to be completed in four years.

All of the people who were to work on the portion of the pipeline from Prudhoe Bay to Glennallen were to be dispatched from union halls located in Fairbanks. Officials estimated that 22,000 workers were to be employed at the peak construction period, some 16,000 of those to be hired out of Fairbanks union halls. In exchange for a no-strike clause, the unions negotiated high wages. As a consequence, high base pay and much overtime yielded paychecks of $1,000 to $1,500 per week for laborers and skilled craftsmen. Fairbanks became the hiring and job termination point and therefore had to accommodate both job seekers and those who were returning from work with big paychecks.

Additionally, Fairbanks became the manage-

ment center for the pipeline project. The Army offered the use of surplus buildings on the North Post of Fort Wainwright, and Alyeska converted these into construction headquarters. More than 500 project management personnel who worked there lived in the Fairbanks community. Furthermore, there also was a pipeline construction camp located on the fort to house workers employed at the Fairbanks pipeyard and along the pipeline running near the town. This camp housed 1,164 workers.

Supplies for the northern segment of the pipeline project were freighted to Fairbanks and then sent north by cargo airplanes before the road to Prudhoe Bay was completed. Fairbanks, as in the old days, served as a transportation and supply center—only on a much larger scale.

Fairbanks also became a service center. Alyeska Pipeline Service Company employed contractors and subcontractors to build the project. Many of these companies established administrative centers in Fairbanks, further expanding the demand for such services as banking, office supplies, telephones, equipment repair, warehousing, and office space.

The A-67 site in 1967 was built on land acquired by the Pioneer Park Board of the Pioneers of Alaska for a Pioneer Memorial Park. It later became Alaskaland. Airport Road and Moore Street cross in the foreground. The U. S. Congress appropriated the money for the construction of Alaskaland, commemorating the 100-year anniversary of the purchase of Alaska from Imperial Russia. Courtesy of Alaskaland

Brigadier General George M. Jones and Colonel Jack F. Riggins, command of the friendly forces in a mock war staged south of Fairbanks, discuss the exercise in front of Riggins's command post. Jones was commander of Fort Wainwright and chief umpire for the ten-day military operation held in February 1967. Courtesy of Fairbanks Daily News-Miner

In 1970 some 45,864 people lived in the 7,361-square mile Fairbanks North Star Borough. The influx of these construction workers and managers and their frenzied activities was to have a profound impact on the region and its residents.

By the end of June 1974 the influx of modern boomers hoping to land a pipeline job had swelled the population of the town. There were only twenty-seven listings under "furnished apartment" in the daily newspaper, with efficiencies renting for $200 per month and two-bedroom apartments going as high as $450. Most restaurants had doubled their prices from the fall of 1973; a cup of soup and a sandwich, for example, at an economical lunch counter cost $2.25. Everywhere there were lines, and it took fifteen to twenty minutes just to drive through the ten-block downtown area at rush hour. At certain times of the day, giant Hercules cargo prop jet planes roared overhead every ten minutes.

One graphic illustration of the dramatic increase in commerce spurred by the beginning of construction on the Trans-Alaska Pipeline was the number of operations at Fairbanks International Airport in 1974 as compared to 1973. In 1973 there were a total of 125,875 landing and take-off operations, of which 60,695 had been logged by the end of June. In 1974, total operations by the end of June had already reached 77,093, with the heaviest air traffic months still ahead. Perhaps even more striking was the increase in the number of air taxi operations and the volume of air cargo handled. Throughout all of 1973, some 24.5 million pounds of freight arrived. Through the end of May, 1974, the total volume of landed freight totaled 23.2 million pounds, nearly equal the total volume of 1973.

Equally impressive was the number of travelers both originating and terminating in Fairbanks. Through May 1973, 48,592 air travelers had terminated their flight in Fairbanks: 62,322 had arrived in the city through May of 1974. Likewise, 47,187 air passengers originated their flights in Fairbanks through May 1973; this number sharply increased to 64,655 through May of 1974.

By the summer of 1975 Fairbanks hummed with activity. Money flowed easily, and aggressive hookers populated Second Avenue—dubbed "Two Street" by the pipeliners—one of the town's main streets. Concentrated within two or three blocks of Second Avenue are most of the town's bars, which remain open until 5 A.M. and reopen a few hours later for early morning drinkers. There are also a few eating establishments and tourist gift shops full of novelties. The Co-op Drug Store, which offers a variety of sundry merchandise and also has a lunch counter, seems to be a gathering place for many of the town's Eskimo and Athapaskan Indian residents and their visiting relatives, who may come from such

Some of the old buildings of Fairbanks were saved after an urban renewal project by moving them to Alaskaland, which was then being developed as A-67, an exposition to celebrate the purchase of Alaska in 1867.

Here, one cabin is in place and another being moved into location. The white building is the original First Presbyterian Church, built in 1904 at Cushman and Seventh Avenue. It formerly had a steeple and vestibule at its right front corner and a large window in the center of the front wall. It was moved to Alaskaland in 1966. In the distance is the riverboat Nenana. Courtesy of Alaskaland

Jim Cassady helped prepare for the Centennial celebration in July 1966. Here, he stands by the wheel of the Lavelle Young, *the sternwheeler that brought E. T. Barnette to the site that became Fairbanks. The wheel is on exhibit at the Pioneer Hall in Alaskaland. Courtesy of* Fairbanks Daily News-Miner

creased crime, and increased unemployment.

At the height of construction, the terminal building and the parking lot at the International Airport were full. Each day the Alaska Airlines Pipeline Express, direct from Houston and Dallas, brought another contingent of "pointy-toes," so called for the cowboy boots many wore. These people were the soldiers of fortune of the oil industry, the professional troubleshooters, drillers, welders, and pipeline layers who have followed their calling from Kuwait to the North Sea, from Africa to Latin America. Motel and hotel rooms in town, if available, cost fifty dollars per night.

Then, as suddenly as the boom had begun, it dropped off. By the summer of 1977 the line had been completed, Alyeska had laid off most of the workers, and the crowds at the airport had thinned considerably. The Fairbanks economy, buoyed by $800,000 a day in wages and purchases during the height of construction, slowed down once again.

At 10:05 A.M. on June 20, 1977, the first oil flowed into the pipeline, nine years after the initial discovery of oil at Prudhoe Bay. The line flowed at an

faraway places as Barrow, Point Hope, Fort Yukon, and Allakaket.

For three hectic years Fairbanks experienced all of the trauma and excitement of pipeline impact, including increased dollars and debts, increased population and deteriorating public services, in-

A street in the gold rush town in Alaskaland in 1967 with some of the old buildings in their new locations. The large log building in the center formerly stood on Fourth Avenue near Cushman. Originally called the Palace Hotel, after it moved to Alaskaland it became a model N. C. Company Store and later was renamed the Pantages Theatre. The false-front building in the center is the old Palfy Sheet Metal Shop, which burned soon after being moved to Alaskaland and was rebuilt as the Palace Saloon. The house with the pillared porch is now the Alaskaland Park office, moved to Fairbanks from Nenana by railroad in 1928. Courtesy of Alaskaland

Amos Wallace, a noted Tlingit carver from southeast Alaska, carved a totem pole during the A-67 opening year. Here he works with an old-style adze for an appreciative young viewer. Courtesy of Alaskaland

initial capacity of 300,000 barrels per day, and the first oil arrived at the Valdez tanker terminal on July 28, 1977. By 1978 oil flowed through the pipeline at a rate of 1.16 million barrels per day. During that first year of operation, 278 million barrels of oil reached Valdez. Today, a total of 1.5 milion barrels of oil is being pushed through the pipeline daily.

In 1974, responding to pressing needs for information and data, the Fairbanks North Star Borough created an Impact Information Center, directed by an Impact Advisory Committee, a group of Fairbanks residents representing the Chamber of Commerce, the Social Concerns Committee, the Borough Assembly, organized labor, Natives, blacks, women— just about every interest group in the community. Meetings were open to the public and the press, and all who so desired could obtain the reports free of charge. In the summer of 1977 the staff of the Impact Information Center issued its final report.

Obviously, the center reports had helped many people. One respondent, for example, had gained a perspective on the community and his relationship to it: "It [the boom] had brought Fairbanks into the modern era in one great wrenching experience instead of gradually, as in most U. S. towns. This dynamicism has encouraged me to stay and be both a participant and an observer in its future growth."

Other respondents gained a perspective on their own personal experiences: "We tend to exaggerate the adverse impacts we expect from a new development and find it difficult to identify what 'impact' consists of after the event occurs. Even though I work for the government, my job was probably easier to get because of the pipeline. But I'm one of the lucky ones. Neither my husband or myself were lured by big money. As a result, we spent the time

together rather than separated for eight weeks at a time."

This respondent experienced many negative as well as positive impacts: "Crowding, inflation, traffic were all hard to bear. Personal, family problems resulted from separation of husband and wife, and long, hard hours. Social life suffered, also due to hours and separation; and crowding, decline in quality and general downtown decay. *But*, we got out of debt, paid off mortgage, saved a little. It was a tradeoff, on balance about equal. But we regretted the loss of a slow paced, friendly Fairbanks—maybe not permanently—and a lifestyle we enjoyed."

And, finally, another resident remarked: "I think the negative influences are more readily traceable to the pipeline—price increases, telephone problems, traffic jams, roads torn up—but as a consumer I've got to admit it's probably also brought us benefits which are less obviously pipeline related—more products and services in particular. I think the dislocation and disruption was in large part transitory, but that the benefits will be with us for years to come, in terms of what we'll be able to do as a state with our pipeline revenues. Looking back, I'd say the negative influences were a small price to pay for the longterm benefits."

By 1978, enough data had been collected to make some comparisons with the pipeline construction and post-construction period. For example, in 1978 an estimated 60,845 residents lived in the borough; in 1977 there had been 69,578, and at the height of construction in 1976 there had been 72,037. On the eve of construction in 1973 there had been an estimated 50,450 residents in the borough. New housing construction decreased by 49 percent in 1978 over 1977, and the papers advertised a total of 978 housing units for rent in January, 1979, and rental costs continued their downward slide through 1978. Fourth quarter 1978 average rents were 4 to 16 percent lower than for the same quarter in 1977. Monthly rental costs for a two-bedroom house dropped to $387 for the fourth quarter of 1978, or 11 percent below the figure for the same period in 1977. In 1976 nonagricultural wage and salary employment came to 26,683 persons; in 1977 it had declined to 22,082; and by 1978 to 21,277.

Oil has increased revenues substantially. In fiscal year 1968, the year of the Prudhoe Bay discovery, the state's general fund revenues amounted to $177,628,000. That amount of money had to suffice to operate the state government. In 1981, the state anticipates general fund revenues of approximately $5 billion, some 90 percent derived from the oil industry. Few anticipated such riches. In

A crew of boat painters poses in front of the Tanana Valley Railroad engine moved to Alaskaland in 1967 from its former location near the railroad station. This engine, designated #1, was among the first used by the Tanana Valley Railroad. Courtesy of Alaskaland

Vice President Hubert Humphrey at A-67 is accompanied by Senator Ernest Gruening (left). Courtesy of Alaskaland

fact, in the 1950s and 1960s oil companies moved mideastern crude oil 8,000 miles to U. S. markets for less than it now costs to move oil from the North Slope to Fairbanks. Oil prices exploded—and with each increase Alaskan revenues benefitted. In December 1978 oil cost $12 per barrel, and had climbed to $36 per barrel in the spring of 1980. In fact, economists began talking about eventual prices of $50 per barrel.

If used wisely, oil revenues, some invested in a permanent fund, will sustain state government spending far into the future. If not, all will be depleted by the time Prudhoe Bay runs dry, sometime early in the twenty first century. Today, the Fairbanks economy is sustained by a number of positive elements: the military (in particular Fort Wainwright), Eielson Air Force Base, Murphy Dome, and, to a lesser extent, the Ballistic Missile Early Warning Station at Clear, Fort Greely at Big Delta, and the military installations at the village of Fort Yukon; the University of Alaska with its large library, research institutes, and rural-oriented programs; the major Athapaskan Indian regional corporation, Doyon Ltd., one of the largest private landholders in North America created by congressional settlement of Alaska's Native claims in 1971; the North Pole refinery and the growing transportation industry, particularly the growing overseas cargo traffic at the international airport; the Alaska Railroad-trucking operations to the North Slope oilfields; and a modest rebirth of placer mining brought about by the phenomenal increase in gold prices in the recent past. Even tourism, a seasonal enterprise, is growing in spite of fairly primitive facilities and fancy prices.

Construction long has contributed to the local economy, but it has varied from year to year, dependent on the vagaries of national, state, and local politics. The service industries have also grown, particularly the health professions. The town boasts of a modern hospital providing about 500 permanent jobs; about ninety physicians are associated with the facility. The Army and Air Force at Fort Wainwright and Eielson Air Force Base also employ military physicians, surgeons, and dentists. More than twenty dentists practice in Fairbanks.

The Fairbanks North Star Borough government provides a wide range of services. For example, it administers a forty-park system covering more than 1,100 acres. Parks offer facilities for baseball, softball, football, track, soccer, skiing, nature trails, picnic areas, day and summer camps. The Fairbanks Recreation Center provides classes in everything from oil painting to pottery as well as well-equipped photographic darkrooms and meeting space for community organizations. Two olympic-sized pools in Fairbanks and North Pole continue to grow in popularity. The Big Dipper complex offers ice skating rinks and tennis courts.

The Noel Wien Library officially opened in the fall of 1977. Beautifully designed and built, it has a book collection of approximately 100,000 volumes and has truly become a community center.

The Fairbanks North Star Borough School District operates nineteen elementary and seven junior and senior high schools and one extensive vocational center with an enrollment of approximately 11,000 students.

The University of Alaska offers rich cultural and recreational opportunities on a year-round basis, and also makes an important contribution to the economic stability of the town. Its 2,312 employees represent 11 percent of the wage and salary employment in Fairbanks. In addition to this direct employment, approximately 740 jobs are generated in the community from the economic activity the University provides to Fairbanks.

In short, Fairbanks has matured from a raw gold mining camp into a small city which offers its residents most of the amenities of modern urban life—but also makes possible superb outdoor recreation opportunities because the wilderness begins on the outskirts of town.

Ruth Barrack (second from right) attended the forty-fifth commencement at the University of Alaska in 1967. She had witnessed all forty-five of the ceremonies held since John Shanley was the only graduate at the first commencement of the Alaska Agricultural College and School of Mines in 1923. At the right is Elmer Rasmuson, president of the Board of Regents from 1957 to 1969 and a member of the board for nineteen years. Mr. and Mrs. Robert Lyle of Anchorage, formerly of Fairbanks, are at the left. Courtesy of Fairbanks Daily News-Miner

The memorial to Carl Ben Eielson was rededicated at Eielson Air Force Base in August 1969. Pictured at the monument are, left to right: General Joseph A. Cunningham, Commander, Alaskan Air Command. Oliver Eielson, Senator Ted Stevens, Elma Eielson Osking, Hannah Eielson Barnord, Arthur Eielson, Congressman Howard Pollock, and Colonel Owen Weddle. Courtesy of Fairbanks Daily News-Miner

Jeff Studdert and Eva McGown on St. Patricks Day in 1967 celebrate with a cake. Mrs. McGown served as the city's official hostess. Jeff Studdert, who was associated with the Independent Lumber Company, promoted and participated in dog mushing. The dog mushing grounds on Farmer's Loop Road are named in his honor. Courtesy of Jeff Studdert Collection, Archives, University of Alaska, Fairbanks

Rosamund Weller in 1971 received recognition from friends, former students, and the community when she retired after thirty-seven years with the school district as a teacher and principal. When she began teaching in 1934, all twelve grades were in the old main school. Andy Miscovich presented Miss Weller with a plaque signifying "a share in our town." Courtesy of Fairbanks Daily News-Miner

The queen contest at the Eskimo Olympics in 1971 featured these contestants in traditional parkas and dress. Left to right: Katherine Itta, Queen Mary Keller, Lillian Venes, and Johanna Harper. Courtesy of Fairbanks Daily News-Miner

Edith Tegoseak from Point Barrow lights the flame of the seal oil lamp to officially open the Eskimo Olympics in August 1969. Courtesy of Fairbanks Daily News-Miner

171

In June 1970 H. A. "Red" Boucher, mayor from 1966 to 1970, was honored with the presentation of a scroll, signed by many Fairbanksans, thanking him for ten years of work with local baseball and for his enthusiasm and effort, which led to the formation of the Goldpanner team. This ceremony took place before the annual Midnight Sun Game at Growden Memorial Park. Boucher shakes hands with shortstop Duane Larson. Next in line is third baseman Dave Roberts. Courtesy of Fairbanks Daily News-Miner

The new terminal facility at the Fairbanks International Airport was completed in 1970. This August night view shows the passenger entrance. Courtesy of Norma Hoyt Collection

The inaugural flight in 1970 by Pan Am of its route from New York to Tokyo with an intermediate stop at Fairbanks included prominent Fairbanksans as well as other Alaskans. From left to right: Howard Pollock, John Holm, Mel Harris, Chuck West, Brad Phillips, Jay Kerttula, John Carlson, Chuck Jensen, unidentified, Ed Orbeck, unidentified, Bill Green, unidentified, Frederick O. Eastaugh, Keith Mather, Duane Snedden. Many Fairbanksans felt that the route finally recognized the importance of Alaska as a crossroads to many parts of the world. Courtesy of John and Edith Holm

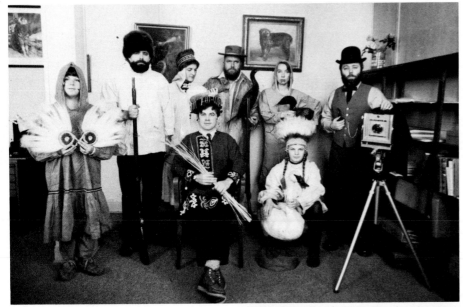

The University Museum staff in 1970 posed in miscellaneous costume for a Christmas card. The solemn group includes, left to right: Loraine Borghorst, George Mueller, Carol Allison, James Greiner, Dinah Larsen, Barry McWayne, Dave Murray (seated), and Mary Pat Wyatt (kneeling). Courtesy of University of Alaska Museum

Jim Greiner, then curator of exhibits at the University of Alaska Museum, is shown with an Eskimo caribou skin house made by Simon Paneak of Anuktuvuk Pass in 1968. The house was constructed for the Institute of Arctic Biology and the museum under Paneak's direction and is now at the museum. A grizzly bear hide was used as a door covering. Courtesy of University of Alaska Museum

In July 1968 Robert Bloom (left), a regent of the University of Alaska from 1921 to 1925, presented Dr. William R. Wood, then president of the university, with a silver cup from his collection of Alaskana. The cup was originally given to John Adelman in 1911 in recognition of the Alaskan wheat he exhibited at the Northwest Land Show in St. Paul, Minnesota. Adelman's farm was the site of the present Hamilton Acres subdivision. L. J. Rowinski, then University of Alaska Museum Director, holds a Russian copper pan used in mining, another item in the Bloom Collection. Courtesy of Fairbanks Daily News-Miner

In 1972 the block of First Avenue between Wickersham and Cowles Streets still held several old buildings. The Masonic Temple building of 1906 is at the left. Next is the Church of Christ, Scientist; farther along stands the First Avenue Bathhouse/Odd Fellows Hall. It was built in 1907 and served as the First Avenue Bathhouse, owned by Cora Madole. Until the pipes froze in the winter of 1909-10, Mrs. Madole lived upstairs, and downstairs was located the clinic of her partner, "Doc" Overgaard. Behind this portion of the building was the bathhouse, a long barn-like structure with a low shed at the back where the boiler was installed. The only entrance to the building was on First Avenue, set back about fifteen feet from the street. A small entry gave access to the health clinic, the stairway, and the bathhouse receiving room. A long hallway extended the length of the building to the boiler shed. Off the hallway were three bathing stalls and a steam room. Shortly after the bathhouse closed, the Odd Fellows purchased the building and converted the bath area into a large hall. In 1963 the Golden North Rebekah Lodge officially purchased the building and continues to maintain the hall. Next is Dr. Sutherland's house, while at the far right is the George C. Thomas Memorial Library of 1909 which is now occupied by North Star Realty and the North Country Federal Credit Union. Courtesy of University of Alaska Museum

This photo shows a happy group at the mining claim. They were, left to right: Mrs. Keith A. Lowell II, a niece of C. J. Berry, an early miner and developer, Peggy Carstens, Keith A. Lowell, II, and "Heine" Carstens.

The Berry Holding Company donated the C. J. Berry Gold Room to the University Museum. The Carstens entertained the Lowells, who were visiting Alaska to attend the opening of the C. J. Berry Gold Room in 1973.

Carstens had come north in 1923 and stayed in Alaska for fifty years, when he made a short visit "Outside." Courtesy of University of Alaska Museum

The Businessmen's Races, sponsored by the Fairbanks Outboard Racing Association, takes off down the Chena River for Nenana in June 1971. The river systems in the Fairbanks area have inspired both serious racing and extensive recreational boating activities. Courtesy of **Fairbanks Daily News-Miner**

Jim Binkley and his son, Skip, licensed river pilots, in front of the flagship **Discovery**'s pilot house. Sternwheeler trips on the Chena and Tanana rivers are a popular way for visitors to see the area and to get a feeling for the old days of river travel in the Interior. Jim Binkley was born in Wrangell in southeastern Alaska where his father operated riverboats on the Stikine River. In 1940 he moved his family to Fairbanks and worked the interior rivers as a licensed pilot. He is the proprietor of Alaska Riverways, Inc., a tourist business. He operates two sternwheelers for cruises on the Chena and Tanana rivers. A versatile man, Jim Binkley also tried his hand at politics and was elected to the state house of representatives, where he served from 1961-1965. Courtesy of **Fairbanks Daily News-Miner**

Charlie Titus, Jim Movius and Toni Movius pose with the trophy for the Yukon 800 race in June 1973. The grueling 800-mile riverboat race on the Tanana and Yukon rivers from Fairbanks to Galena was won by Movius in 1973, 1977, and 1979. He set the course record in 1979 with a time of 14 hours and 1 minute. He was the navigator for Ed Gustafson's winning boat in 1981, Gustafson's third win in the race. *Courtesy of* Fairbanks Daily News-Miner

The Tanana Raft Classic was a springtime event for a few years. In 1971 a contingent of rafts of every sort left the campground at the end of the Chena Pump Road for the day-long trip to Nenana. The campground is close to the site of the old town of Chena, a former rival to Fairbanks which has now completely vanished. *Courtesy of* Fairbanks Daily News-Miner

Paul Gavora (left) is presented with the "Alaskan Small Businessman of the Year" award by Morris Carpenter of the Small Business Administration at a Chamber of Commerce luncheon in May 1972. Since then, Gavora has continued to develop his business interests in Fairbanks and North Pole. *Courtesy of* Fairbanks Daily News-Miner

Fire destroyed the Nordale Hotel, a venerable landmark, in February 1972. The building on Second Avenue had been remodeled with a new facade of metal panels, but the old wooden building burned rapidly. Lost in the fire was Eva McGown, who had served as a hostess for the city for many years and who made her home in the hotel. Courtesy of Fairbanks Daily News-Miner

Dorothy Wrede serves punch during the 1976 Golden Days to, left to right: Elizabeth Burdick, Lola Tilley, and Vide Bartlett. Mrs. Tilley was head of the University of Alaska Department of Home Economics for many years. Mrs. Bartlett was the widow of E. L. "Bob" Bartlett, who served as Alaska's delegate to Congress and later as Alaska's senior U.S. Senator. Courtesy of Fairbanks Daily News-Miner

Sylvia Ringstad and Katerine Anderson wait patiently for the arrival of Gerald Ford, who visited Fairbanks in December 1975. Mrs. Ringstad was on the city council for twenty one years and Mayor of Fairbanks in 1965-66 after a distinguished career in business and raising a family in Fairbanks. Mrs. Ringstad was Fairbanks's Mother of the Year in 1952. Courtesy of Fairbanks Daily News-Miner

Dick Underwood was the poultry and rabbit superintendent at the fair in 1973. His son, Jim, carries food for some of the rabbits. Courtesy of Tanana Valley Fair Association

Four university presidents at the inauguration of Dr. Robert W. Hiatt as president, May 1974. From left to right: Mrs. Katrina Moore, President Emeritus Terris Moore, Mrs. Virginia Patty, President Emeritus Ernest Patty, Mrs. Dorothy Jane Wood, President William R. Wood, Mrs. Bess Hiatt, and incoming president Robert W. Hiatt. Courtesy of Archives, University of Alaska, Fairbanks

Four former Chamber of Commerce managers got together for this 1975 photo. Left to right: Ross Miller, Don Dickey, Wally Baer, and R. A. "Dutch" Derr. Dickey for many years was director of the State Chamber of Commerce and in 1981 became director of the State Division of Tourism. Courtesy of Fairbanks Daily News-Miner

In 1972 the Frank Miller house, built in 1923, still stood across from the railroad station on North Cushman. It was dismantled in 1981. The Wayfarer Hotel was a barracks-like building that is now gone. Frank Miller owned a number of bars and restaurants including the original "Miner's Home," which was a favorite of W. F. Thompson, Fairbanks's well-known early newspaperman. Courtesy of University of Alaska Museum

Lee Wareham, Harry Reimer, and Dave Brennen were members of the North Star Borough assembly in 1980. Here, they listed attentively to a citizens group. Courtesy of Fairbanks Daily News-Miner

The Hamme Pool, administered by the Department of Parks and Recreation of the Fairbanks North Star Borough, opened in 1977, is used by the community for recreation and swimming instruction. The school district teaches many pupils from the public schools. This recreational swim was taken in August 1979. Courtesy of Fairbanks Daily News-Miner

Jo Scott, who has been involved in music and arts activities in Fairbanks for many years, prepares for her summer camp in 1979. Photograph by Teri De'ak; courtesy of Alaska Association for the Arts

Paul Rosenthal, well-known violinist and founder of the Sitka Music Festival, is shown performing during Paul Rosenthal Week in Fairbanks, April 1979. Photograph by Steve Stolee; courtesy of Alaska Association for the Arts

The Woodwind Workshop performed in 1979 at the Mainstage Fairbanks, summer series sponsored by the Alaska Association for the Arts. Members of the group are, left to right: Richard Tremarello, Candis Shannon, Sheila D. Hille, Dorli McWayne, and Ted DeCorso. Fairbanks supports many municipal groups including the University of Fairbanks Symphony and Alaska Brass. Photograph by Steve Stolee; courtesy of Alaska Association for the Arts

Two popular performers at the Time Out at Noon programs sponsored by the Alaska Association for the Arts are Sally Smith and Ron Inouye, photographed during the 1980 season. The programs are held throughout the summer at the new Borough Library. Smith is a Fairbanks representative to the Alaska state legislature. Courtesy of Alaska Association for the Arts

The Pearl Creek Recorder Consort in 1979 consisted of, left to right: Mimi Chapin, Walt Herreid, Bucky Wilson, and Teri Viereck. Photograph by Steve Stolee; courtesy of Alaska Association for the Arts

Tourism is a major industry in Fairbanks, and one of the stops on the local bus tours is the new University Museum which opened in 1979. An Alaskan Highway Tour bus was among the first to bring visitors to the new facility. Courtesy of University of Alaska Museum

The Tanana Valley Fair is one of the major summer events in the Interior. Every other year it is the Alaska State Fair. Crowds increase every year. Here they fill the midway in the mid-1970s. Photo by Lens Unlimited. Courtesy of Tanana Valley Fair Association

In 1978 the North American Sled Dog Races started in downtown Fairbanks. Second Avenue was blocked off and an eager crowd lined the street. The south side (right) of Second Avenue has only the Empress Theatre building of 1927, now the Co-op Drug Store to remind us of old Fairbanks. The space beyond it, now a parking lot, was the site of the Nordale Hotel, which burned in 1972. Courtesy of Fairbanks Daily News-Miner

The giant cabbage exhibit and contest is a popular event at the fair. This entry in 1976 is admired by Rachel Mullen (left) and Evelyn Clark. Courtesy of Tanana Valley Fair Association

This view, looking down at the Cushman Street Bridge, was taken May 9, 1968. The new J. C. Penney store is prominent in the upper center while the N. C. Company buildings are facing the river in the center-right. This view shows how some of the old N. C. buildings had been joined to create the large building that now houses Nordstrom department store. Courtesy of Fairbanks Daily News-Miner

Irene Sherman and Harold Gillam inspect the newly completed Golden Towers building in December 1976. The building provides apartments for senior citizens in downtown Fairbanks. Gillam was mayor of Fairbanks from 1972 to 1978. Courtesy of Fairbanks Daily News-Miner

The Fairbanks Womens Club was long an active participant in community affairs. The club gradually disbanded, but the last few active members gathered in 1981 to donate a final grant of $1,700.50 to the University of Alaska Annual Fund, where it will serve as part of the endowment for the Talent Grant program.

Left to right: Eleanor Burnham, Irene Brooks, Brynhild Nordin, Emalie Avakoff, and Ella Pierson. Seated is Marge Lockwood. Not present but active in bringing about the donation was Lydia Fohn-Hansen. Courtesy of Evy Walters

1981 Fair Board, left to right: Rudy Domke, Anne Luick, Dennis Cook, Hal Livingston, Dave McNary, Ruth Stratton, Becky Kuryla, Louis Stockwell. Missing is Sandy Havrefield. Courtesy of Tanana Valley Fair Association

A torchlight parade down Second Avenue during the March 1979 Ice Carnival. Courtesy of **Fairbanks Daily News-Miner**

Poldine Carlo, an Athapaskan woman and author, tends the Eskimo lamp during the annual World Eskimo-Indian Olympics in August 1980. These Olympics bring together people from all parts of Alaska, northern Canada, and Greenland to compete in Native games and feats of skills. The traditional lamp, loaned each year by the University of Alaska Museum, must be tended carefully to produce a constant, uniform light. Courtesy of **Fairbanks Daily News-Miner**

Clara Rust, whose memories of old Fairbanks made community history immediate to people, celebrated her eightieth birthday at the Pioneer Home. Her family from Alaska and Seattle gathered with her. From left: Cora Saunders, a daughter; Larry Chesley, grandson; Barbara Rust, daughter-in-law; Clara Rust; Lila Cox, daughter; June Sidars, daughter; Susan Berry, granddaughter; and Mary Cordes, head housekeeper for the Pioneer Home. **This Old House**, by Mrs. Rust and Jo Ann Wold, recounts Mrs. Rust's life in early Fairbanks. Courtesy of **Fairbanks Daily News-Miner**

The annual Christmas party at the Fairbanks Pioneer Home in 1969 was its usual success. Sig Wold served as Santa Claus and presented presents to Julia "Cookie" Seltenreich. Adriana Coyle and Dorothy King look on. Many of the presents were donated by Fairbanks merchants. Courtesy of **Fairbanks Daily News-Miner**

Harvey Marlin and Tillie Link, King and Queen Regents for the 1979 Golden Days, at the Pioneer Mug-up at the new Eagles Hall danced till the night was done. Marlin was ninety-one years old at the time. The two old Fairbanks neighbors seem to typify the spirit of the city, which ages with vitality. All-Alaska Weekly photograph by Coleen Redman

Bruce Thomas, Jack Linck, and Slim Moore at the Pioneer's Convention in Anchorage in 1977. Courtesy of Evolyn Melville Collection

Fox Spring, near the junction of the Steese and Elliot highways near the old townsite of Fox is a source of water for many who claim it is the best water in the Fairbanks area. Winter and summer, people line up to fill their jugs and cans. The spring and rest area are maintained by the Alaska State Division of Lands. Courtesy of Fairbanks Daily News-Miner

The plaza in front of the Civic Center at Alaskaland is the scene for a Boy Scouts Youth Winter Fair in the spring of 1974. The Civic Center houses a theatre, exhibit hall, and art galleries. The steamer Nenana, at the right, is registered as a National Historic Site. Courtesy of Alaska Association for the Arts

At the 1978 North American Open Dog Sled Race on Second Avenue, Roger Reitano races his dogs past a crowd in the downtown area. Courtesy of Fairbanks Daily News-Miner

The Skiathon, a major cross-country event, starts on a frosty March morning in 1972 up the hill behind the Beluga, an air-supported structure on the University of Alaska campus. Courtesy of Fairbanks Daily News-Miner

The size of the Fairbanks Daily News-Miner *staff in 1979 had passed anything W. F. Thompson could have imagined. The staff includes, left to right in the first row: C. W. Snedden, board chairman and publisher; Duane Snedden, assistant publisher; Richard Burley, manager, Commercial Printing; Dwight Foster, advertising manager; G. Kent Sturgis, managing editor; Al Anthon, commercial artist; Evelyn Sikes, classified advertising supervisor; and Dalton Haslett, classified ad manager (since retired). Courtesy of* Fairbanks Daily News-Miner

The News-Miner *newsroom in 1979 with the new video display terminal system. Courtesy of* Fairbanks Daily News-Miner

The Trans-Alaska pipeline is connected as it crosses the Yukon River bridge north of Fairbanks. Fairbanks was a focal point for pipeline construction since the bridge and the Dalton Highway made Fairbanks a supply center for traffic to the north. Courtesy of* Fairbanks Daily News-Miner

The University of Alaska campus in 1979 was modern and attractive with almost no visible signs of its early days. The cornerstone of the old Main building stands in the plaza, and Dr. Bunnell's house is relocated among the faculty houses where it serves as a nursery school. The Fairbanks campus has nearly 4,000 students and 340 full-time faculty members involved in over eighty areas of study. Research institutes and centers are concentrated on the West Ridge, where the Geophysical Institute towers above the other buildings. The large buildings in the upper-center are dormitories. Fairbanks is the only residential campus in the university's statewide system. *Photograph by Sabra McCracken; courtesy of University of Alaska, Fairbanks*

This aerial view about 1980 shows the newly completed Steese Highway bypass running along the Chena River and the new Federal Building in the lower left. The river winds past the taller buildings of downtown Fairbanks and out toward the University of Alaska in the distance. At the lower right are the houses in Island Homes. Courtesy of Fairbanks Daily News-Miner

John Butrovich, for many years a member of the Alaska Territorial and then State Senate, was a speaker at the dedication of the North Pole Refinery in October 1977. The construction of the refinery was made possible by the completion of the Trans-Alaska Pipeline. The refinery taps into the pipeline for supplies of crude oil. The facility is located in the community of North Pole, eleven miles south of Fairbanks. Courtesy of Fairbanks Daily News-Miner

Boswell, John C. *History of Alaskan Operations of United States Smelting, Refining, and Mining Company,* Fairbanks, Alaska: University of Alaska, Mineral Industries Research Laboratory, 1979.

Bowen, B. L. *The Economic Impact of the Military on Alaska,* M. A. Thesis, University of Alaska, Fairbanks, 1970.

Cashen, William R. *Farthest North College President: Charles E. Bunnell and the Early History of the University of Alaska,* Fairbanks, Alaska: University of Alaska Press, 1972.

Cole, Terrence. *E. T. Barnette: The Strange Story of the Man Who Founded Fairbanks,* Anchorage, Alaska: Alaska Northwest Publishing Company, 1981.

Cooley, Richard A. *Fairbanks, Alaska: A Survey of Progress,* Juneau, Alaska: Alaska Development Board, July 1954

Dixon, Mim. *What Happened to Fairbanks? The Effects of the Trans-Alaska Oil Pipeline on the Community of Fairbanks, Alaska,* Boulder, Colorado: Westview Press, 1978.

The Fairbanks Commercial Club. *Descriptive of Fairbanks: Alaska's Golden Heart,* Fairbanks, Alaska, April 1916.

Fison, Susan R., and Cindy L. Quisenberry. *Fairbanks North Star Borough Impact Information Center Final Report, 1977,* Chapter XV, Impact Center Evaluation and Attitudes of Readers, Fairbanks, Alaska, 1977.

Fried, Neal. *The Economic Impact of the University of Alaska on Fairbanks,* Community Research Center, Special Report No. 8, Fairbanks, Alaska, November 1980.

Halevi, Marcus, and Kenneth Andrasko. *Alaska Crude: Visions of the Last Frontier,* Boston-Toronto: Little, Brown, 1977.

Hunt, William R., *North of 53°: The Wild Days of the Alaska-Yukon Mining Frontier 1870-1914.* New York and London: MacMillan Publishing Co., Inc., 1974.

Michael, Henry N., editor, *Lieutenant Zagoskin's Troubles in Russian America, 1842-1844: The First Ethnographic and Geographic Investigations in the Yukon and Kuskokibim Valleys of Alaska.* Toronto, Canada: University of Toronto Press for the Arctic Institute of North America, 1967.

Naske, Claus-M. *Edward Lewis Bob Bartlett of Alaska: A Life in Politics,* Fairbanks, Alaska: University of Alaska Press, 1979.

Naske, Claus-M., and Herman E. Slotnick. *Alaska: A History of the 49th State,* Grand Rapids, Michigan: William B. Eerdmans, 1979.

Orth, Donald. *Dictionary of Alaska Place Names,* U. S. Geological Service Professional Paper No. 567, Washington, D.C.: Government Printing Office, 1967.

Potter, Jean. *The Flying North,* Sausalito, California: Comstock Editions, 1977.

Rickard, T. A. *Through the Yukon and Alaska,* San Francisco: Mining and Scientific Press, 1909.

Rogers, George W., and Richard A. Cooley. *Alaska's Population and Economy: Regional Growth, Development, and Future Outlook,* College, Alaska: Institute of Business, Economic, and Government Research, University of Alaska, 1963, Vol. II, Statistical Handbook.

Solka, Paul, Jr., and Art Bremer. *Adventures in Alaska Journalism Since 1903: Fairbanks Daily News-Miner,* Fairbanks, Alaska: Commercial Printing Co., October 1980.

United States Army, Alaska. *The Army's Role in the Building of Alaska,* Headquarters, United States Army, Alaska: Public Information Office, Pamphlet 360-5, April 1969.

Articles

Adams, C. W. "I hauled 'Fairbanks' on a Sternwheeler," *Alaska Sportsman,* September 1961, pp. 14-15.

"An Empire Out of Wilderness," *The Fairbanks Timers,* Industrial Edition, April 3, 1910, pp. 1-28.

Bruce, Julia M. "Schools of the Tanana Valley," *Alaska-Yukon Magazine,* January 1909, pp. 263-76.

Community Information Center, "Community Information Review: 1978 Year-End Wrap-Up," March 1979, pp. 1-14.

Davis, Edby. "Alaska as I Knew It," *Alaska Sportsman,* October 1964, pp. 26-29, 55-57; November 1964, pp. 16-19; December 1964, pp. 30-32.

Koenig, Duane. "Ghost Railway in Alaska: The Story of the Tanana Valley Railroad," *Pacific Northwest Quarterly,* January 1954, pp. 8-12.

Metheany, B. B. "Men and Endeavor in the Tanana Valley," *Alaska-Yukon Magazine,* January 1909, pp. 289-327.

Spring Abe. "Early History of the Tanana Valley," *Alaska-Yukon Magazine,* January 1909, pp. 259-62.

Index

Fairbanks, Alaska. – October 1915.